More Praise for Christian Felber

'The Economy for the Common Good has demonstrated an ability to draw together a partnership of companies, consumers and communities... by offering a fresh alternative.'

Bruce Watson, *Guardian*

'We need an entirely new economic system if we are to avert collapse, and Christian Felber points the way. This path-breaking, optimistic book shows that it is possible to have an economy that serves us rather than enslaving us.'

Richard Heinberg, Author of *The End of Growth*

'Offers a clear analysis that combines pragmatic designs for some of the potential institutions of the next system with a strategy for building a movement that can bring these institutions into being. An important contribution to an essential global conversation.'

Gar Alperovitz, Author of *America Beyond Capitalism*

'Through the example of the Economy for the Common Good, everyone can see that doing business on the basis of a transparent, holistic, value and stakeholder oriented approach is possible. These ethical goals are indispensable for a humane future on this planet.'

Lisa Muhr, Co-founder of the
Goddess of Fortune Fashion Collective

Christian Felber is an Austrian alternative economist and university lecturer. He is an internationally renowned speaker, author of several award-winning bestsellers and a regular commentator on ethics, business and economics in various media. He co-founded the NGO Attac Austria and initiated the Economy for the Common Good as well as the planned Bank for the Common Good, which will be Austria's first ethical finance institute.

CHANGE
EVERYTHING

Creating an Economy for the Common Good

CHRISTIAN FELBER

Translated by Susan Nurmi

With a Foreword by Eric Maskin

Zed Books

LONDON

Change Everything: Creating an Economy for the Common Good
was first published in English in 2015 by Zed Books Ltd,
Unit 2.8 The Foundry, 17 Oval Way, London SE11 5RR, UK

Originally published in German in 2012 under the title
Die Gemeinwohl-Ökonomie. Aktualisierte und erweiterte Neuausgabe
by Paul Zsolnay Verlag, Wien, Austria

www.zedbooks.co.uk

Copyright © Deuticke im Paul Zsolnay Verlag, Wien 2012

The right of Christian Felber to be identified as the author
of this work has been asserted by him in accordance with
the Copyright, Designs and Patents Act, 1988

Typeset in Adobe Garamond Pro by seagulls.net
Index: John Barker
Cover designed by www.alice-marwick.co.uk
Printed and bound by CPI Group (UK) Ltd, Croydon, CR0 4YY

A catalogue record for this book is available from the British Library

ISBN 978-1-78360-473-9 hb
ISBN 978-1-78360-472-2 pb
ISBN 978-1-78360-474-6 pdf
ISBN 978-1-78360-475-3 epub
ISBN 978-1-78360-476-0 mobi

MIX
Paper from
responsible sources
FSC
www.fsc.org   FSC® C013604

For the Common Good!

CONTENTS

ACKNOWLEDGEMENTS

I wish to express my thanks to the countless individuals who have committed themselves to the further development, dissemination and implementation of the model for an Economy for the Common Good and created a global "energy field" which is continuously gaining in momentum. These are private persons, entrepreneurs, organizers of events, academics, journalists, public speakers and supporters of various kinds. I specifically wish to thank:

... Joachim Sikora, who coined the German term for Economy for the Common Good, *Gemeinwohl-Ökonomie*, years ago, using it in reference to a reform-oriented economic model (www.joachimsikora. de); Stefano Zamagni and Luigino Bruni, the Italian authors of *L'Economia del bene comune*, and Herman Daly and John B. Cobb Jr., the American authors of *For the Common Good*. This convergence of similar approaches and concepts shows that the time is more than ripe for an Economy for the Common Good!

... the numerous people who read the manuscript and contributed their ideas, among them Christian Apl, Jean-Philippe Baum, Harro Colshorn, Christian Fischer, Andreas Giselbrecht, Ludmilla Groß, Günter Grzega, Sophie Gudenus, Astrid Hafner, Gus Hagelberg, Gisela Heindl, Christian Hiß, Lutz Knakrügge, Jörg Knall, Franziska Kohler, Katharina Kronsteiner, Erwin Leitner, Christian Loy, Marita Matschke, Lisa Muhr, Sonia Niżnik, Isabell Popescu, Alfred Racek, Emanuel Raviola, Andrea Reitinger, Christian Rüther, Barbara Stefan, Eva Stilz, Subhash, Rahel Sophia Süß, Rita Trattnig, Jörg-Arolf Wittig, Wilhelm Zwirner ...

… the very fine and professional team at Deuticke-Verlag which worked together with Bettina Wörgötter, Susanne Rössler, Annette Lechner, Brigitte Kaserer, Peter Guttmann and Martina Schmidt. And in the same way Ken Barlow and the whole team at Zed Books who as a workers' collective already live many of the values proposed in this book.

… the translator Susan Nurmi, who has done an excellent job and conveyed the meaning of every single word.

… Gus Hagelberg, who is coordinating the dissemination of the Economy for the Common Good in the Anglo-Saxon world and has contributed decisively to the success of this book.

… Diego Isabel La Moneda from the Spanish movement who introduced the ECG in Buckingham Palace to representatives from 41 British associations.

… Eric Maskin who has contributed an equally precise and humane foreword.

… Cornelius Pietzner, who is helping me as a personal coach and also with funding of the translation costs.

… all those people who have reflected on solidarity-oriented, democratic and sustainable ways of doing business, contributed to the discussion concerning them and/or practise them in their daily lives.

… Gaia and Pachamama, custodians of the Common Good.

FOREWORD

Christian Felber thinks big. Not content with marginal change, he proposes a thorough overhaul of our capitalist system. In his world, companies still earn profits. But they are driven not by revenues and costs, but by their Common Good balance sheet, which evaluates them on how cooperative they are with other companies, whether their products and services satisfy human needs, and how humane their working conditions are. A company is awarded Common Good points accordingly, and its score is published, so that customers know whom they are dealing with. A good score also entitles the company to favourable government treatment: lower taxes, better borrowing terms and more public contracts.

Could this world actually come about? I honestly don't know. But I have encountered such a society on a smaller scale. Thirteen years ago, I was introduced to the Camphill movement, which builds communities where disabled people live together with their caregivers (my son lived at a Camphill school for six years). Like Christian's utopia, these communities place the highest value on cooperation, dignity and service. If they can do it, perhaps Christian's vision is not so far-fetched.

Eric Maskin

PREFACE

TAPAS: There are plenty of alternatives

On 6 October 2010, a process of change began in Vienna: the Economy for the Common Good took its first step towards turning an idea into a movement. It all began with a dozen Austrian enterprises; four years later, the list of supporters included some 1,700 enterprises and 200 organizations. Schools and universities from different parts of Europe and across the entire Latin American continent are now participating. Local chapters (also known as "energy fields") are being founded in more and more countries, forming the backbone of the movement. Associations are coordinating developmental tasks, and expert teams are giving support to economic, political and cultural pioneers. The Economy for the Common Good was instigated by the activist organization Attac Austria, which I co-founded in 2000 and remained active in until 2014. In addition to teaching duties at the Vienna University of Economics and Business, book-writing and international lecture tours, I have since devoted my political energy and creativity to building up an international Economy for the Common Good movement and establishing the Bank for the Common Good project in Austria.

In the same week when the original German-language edition of this book came out in August 2010, the renowned Bertelsmann Foundation published a survey which found that 88 percent of respondents in Germany expressed the desire for a new economic order. In Austria, an even larger proportion of the interviewees expressed this sentiment, namely 90 percent. Just imagine: 90 percent articulated a conscious desire for an economic model other than the currently prevailing one. This is surely unprecedented, isn't it? At lectures, audiences have given similar responses. More and more people are realizing that we are not currently experiencing an *isolated* financial crisis; they can see that financial bubbles, unemployment and various types of crises – income and wealth distribution, climate, energy, hunger and consumption, as well as crises of meaning, values and democracy – are all inherently connected and symptoms of a comprehensive systemic problem. In the capitalistic market economy means are confused with goals; a model which is devoid of meaning is becoming obsolete.

And yet in part, the representatives of the people still claim "There is no alternative". This dictum, uttered by Margaret Thatcher, is still popular among a powerful elite which obstruct change. But in a democracy alternatives always exist. One of the main objectives of this book is to demonstrate, in concrete terms, that there are in fact alternatives to the current economic order.

The decisive question is: which direction should be taken? Should the economy become more ecological and sustainable; should it become a "post-growth economy"? Should it become more regional and more resilient on the basis of bio-regions and transition towns? Should the welfare state be strengthened and inequality be limited as in the familiar "social market economy"? Should the focus move from competition to cooperation in the name of a solidarity-based economy? Should priority be given to human dignity and should every individual be granted the right of co-determination to achieve a higher degree of economic democracy?

The response of the Economy for the Common Good is that all of these values should be realized to a greater degree than they are today. And the common denominator is "the common good". This concept was not invented by us; it stems from a long tradition. The term *bonum commune* was coined by Thomas Aquinas in the thirteenth century. Since then it has run like a common thread through Christian social doctrine – and through the constitutions of democratic states. German Basic Law states: "Property entails responsibility. Its use is also to serve the welfare of the general public." According to Italy's constitution, "public and private economic activity should be oriented to the common good". The Constitution of Bavaria is the most unequivocal in this regard, stating: "All economic activity serves the common good."

This was even the view taken in ancient Greece. Aristotle distinguished between the healthy *oikonomia*, in which money serves as a means for the "good life", and the unnatural *chrematistike*, in which multiplication of money becomes a means in itself.[1]

What all great concepts have in common is their enormous attraction. Various protagonists and regimes co-opt them for their own objectives and interests. Hitler misappropriated the concept of the common good, and socialist dictatorships have taken possession of it as well. But that should not preclude perpetuating what remains a coherent and apt concept. We do not eliminate the concepts of "freedom", "truthfulness" and "love" from our vocabulary just because they get misused. The best concepts run the highest risk of usurpation. And the more valuable a concept is, the more vehement will be the wrangling about how to define it. This makes the democratic deliberation necessary for promoting its realization all the more crucial.

THE PROCESS OF PARTICIPATION – AN OPEN-ENDED DEVELOPMENT

Two crucial questions pose themselves: what does the "common good" mean and who defines it? As a guiding concept, the Economy for the Common Good has no preconceived meaning except that it signifies how important the well-being of all human beings and the natural world is. "The greatest happiness for the greatest number of people" – this utilitarian principle which we are all familiar with falls short because the value, and hence dignity, of all human beings is equal. The only immanent meaning of the common good concept is that everyone's well-being counts. Otherwise the concept constitutes nothing more than an umbrella term in the sense of a constitutional goal which sums up the key values of democratic societies. The precise meaning of its individual components can and should be determined democratically. The "common good" is neither divinely handed down nor does it derive from the grace of any emperor. This, in turn, implies two things:

1. The conceptual cornerstones of the Economy for the Common Good must be discussed by a large number of people in the course of a comprehensive developmental process before they can be incorporated into a clear-cut democratic process. What this essentially involves is establishing a new economic order in democratic terms. The core elements of the model outlined in this book do not constitute a final result, but rather a point of departure for developing such a new order!

2. If the democratic process develops in accordance with our ideal notions, several years from now directly elected economic conventions will have drafted a section of the constitution concerning the economy, and the population will have accepted it using an innovative voting procedure. Needless to say, the model will continue to remain open-ended – for the very reason that ongoing democratic renegotiation of our societal "guiding light" forms the core of the common good.

THREE KEY CONCERNS

The Economy for the Common Good has three major focuses:

1. It strives to dissolve the contradiction between those values held by business and those held by society by finding ways to reward, in business, the values that allow us to nurture interpersonal relationships. These include the building of trust, mutual appreciation, cooperation, connectedness with nature, solidarity and sharing.

2. The values and goals laid down in our constitutions should be systematically implemented in business practices. The currently existing economic order, which has been constituted by the system itself, diametrically contradicts the spirit of many political constitutions or parts thereof.

3. The approach to measuring economic success should move from evaluating the *means* to assessing the *goals* of business, operating on the premise that the purpose of all business is not to maximize profit, but rather to promote the common good. In other words: exchange values do not constitute the goal, use values do. Human beings derive their means of subsistence from use values alone. Exchange values are only useful indirectly, not inherently. Money can neither nourish me, nor warm me, nor embrace me. The Economy for the Common Good wants to measure what really counts. The Common Good Product would replace the GDP, the Common Good Balance Sheet would supplement the financial balance sheet, and the ethical return on investment would displace the financial return as the primary parameter of economic success.

One-sided measurement of success in terms of monetary indicators has played a major role in turning economics into a lifeless science.

In my eyes the Czech economist Tomáš Sedláček has found the best metaphor to date for conveying what has happened to the field of economic science: "If the soul is torn out of an organism, what remains is a zombie."[2] Classical economics has no soul; hence it poses a great threat to a human, sustainable society. We must breathe a soul into it again. This healing process would begin with the act of re-embedding the economy into our cultural value system, thus ending the ethical schizophrenia created by the chasm between business and society. And it would go so far as to re-embed both economic thought and practice into the planetary ecosphere.

ONE ALTERNATIVE AMONG MANY

The Economy for the Common Good does not say "This is the only conceivable economic model for the future". Rather it describes important elements of an economic order: goals, values, success parameters, markets, gainful employment, ownership, financial systems and others. It is neither comprehensive nor closed. In fact it strives to be combined with other alternatives and to be enriched by them. Classic "friends" of the Economy for the Common Good are: the solidarity-based economy, the commons, economic democracy, B Corporations, social business, shared value, economic subsidiarity, the gift economy, and the post-growth economy, to name but a few. It would not even be advisable for one model to assert itself over all the others; instead it would be desirable to have the most appealing, consensual components of various alternative approaches combined in a participatory process in search of a democratic economic order.

In Great Britain much has already been accomplished in the direction of exploring such alternatives. Schumacher College, the New Economics Foundation and the Findhorn Community are some of the beacons in this alternative landscape. Tim Jackson and the Skidelskys are perpetuating the pioneering endeavours of E. F. Schumacher as well as those of the American Herman Daly. One of the world's largest enterprises owned by its employees is located in Britain: the John Lewis Partnership. And the publisher of this book, Zed Books, is a workers' collective.

As of late 2014, this book was available in seven languages; in addition to this English-language edition, publication of Serbian- and Dutch-language versions are planned for 2015. Thus the book will soon be available in ten languages and can finally be distributed worldwide. In addition to readers in Britain and the USA, people in countries extending from Moldova to India and from Kenya to Canada have expressed interest in an English-language version.

THE STRUCTURE OF THE BOOK

A short crisis analysis of the current economic (dis-)order is given in Chapter 1, followed in Chapter 2 by an extensive explication of the core of the Economy for the Common Good. Chapters 3 and 4 deal with the financial system (the "democratic bank") and property, which are two pillars of the Economy for the Common Good. Chapter 5, entitled "Motivation and meaning", addresses "softer" issues, exploring the apprehension held by many that the incentive to perform would be lost in an ethical market economy. Chapter 6 is devoted entirely to democracy. As I maintain, the Economy for the Common Good can only be implemented comprehensively in the framework of a direct and participatory democracy which is more advanced than the current post-democracy. Chapter 7 shows examples of already-existing common-good-oriented enterprises and activities. Chapter 8 sketches out the strategies of the four-year-old movement and reports on its current state of development. The book concludes with two appendices: the first answers a larger series of FAQs (frequently asked questions) raised by hundreds of people who have attended lectures in many countries; the second contains a 20-point summary, which could conceivably serve as a compendium for an economic convention.

Participation in an economic convention is one of numerous possibilities for contributing to an Economy for the Common Good. This book pursues three objectives: (1) It strives to offer a clear and consistent full-scale alternative to the prevailing economic order. (2) It sketches out a concrete procedure of democratic implementation which leaves the model open for combination and cooperation with other alternatives at the same time – in keeping with the motto "There are plenty of alternatives!" (3) It offers each and every person, each and every enterprise, each and every body politic and each and every educational institution concrete and low-threshold possibilities for participating in and shaping the transition to a new economic order. Help us shape it![3]

ONE
A BROKEN SYSTEM

Cooperating, helping others and ensuring that
justice prevails is a basic, biologically rooted human
motivation which is found all over the globe. This pattern
manifests itself beyond all cultural boundaries.[1]
Joachim Bauer

HUMAN VALUES – VALUES OF THE ECONOMY

It's peculiar: although values are meant to offer basic orientation,
serving as the "guiding lights" of our lives, the values which hold for
the economy today are completely different from those which apply
to our daily interpersonal relationships. In regard to our friendships
and everyday relationships, we thrive when we live in accordance with
human values: the building of trust, honesty, esteem, respect, empathy,
cooperation, mutual help and sharing. The "free" market economy is
based on the rules of the systematic pursuit of profit and competition.
These pursuits promote egoism, greed, avarice, envy, ruthlessness and
irresponsibility. This contradiction is not merely a blemish in a complex
or multivalent world; rather, it is a cultural catastrophe; it divides us
inwardly – as individuals and as a society.

VALUES ARE GUIDING LIGHTS

The contradiction is fatal because values are the foundation of communal life. We set life goals and orient our actions according to them, investing them with meaning. In Spanish the word "sentido" denotes meaning as well as direction. Values are like a guiding light which gives the road of life direction. But if our guiding light for daily life points in an ethical direction – towards building of trust, cooperation, sharing – and suddenly, in a partial realm of life, namely the market economy, a second "guiding light" points in the opposite direction – in the direction of egoism, competition, greed – then we are plagued by a terrible quandary: should we act in the spirit of solidarity and cooperation, help each other and always be mindful of everyone's welfare? Or should we always look to our own advantage first and short-change others as our competitors? The direness of the conflict lies in the fact that legislators favour the false guiding light, thus promoting values that we all suffer from. This does not necessarily become evident immediately because no law says that you should be egoistic, greedy, avaricious, ruthless and irresponsible. But what the law does say is that we should pursue financial profit in business and compete with one another. This is reflected in numerous laws, regulations and treaties of nation-states, the European Union (EU) and the World Trade Organization (WTO). The result is an epidemic emergence of antisocial behaviour in business – because these kinds of behaviours lead to entrepreneurial "success".

TURNING EGOISM INTO COMMON GOOD

The "imperative" that we should compete in business and pursue the largest possible amount of personal financial gain (i.e. behave egoistically) stems from the paradoxical hope that the good of all will result from the egoistic behaviour of the individual. This ideology was established 250 years ago by Adam Smith, the first major national economist. Smith literally said: "It is not from the benevolence of the butcher, the brewer, or the baker that we expect our dinner, but from their regard to their own interest."[2]

My aim is not to berate Smith. At the time it was an understandable notion. The pursuit of self-interest on the part of "individuals" was new; "enterprises" were primarily tiny and powerless and, in addition, locally integrated and personally responsible. In many cases company founder, proprietor, employer and employee were still united in one person (the baker, the carpenter, etc.). There was no free movement of capital, there were no anonymous global corporations, no multi-billion-dollar investment funds.

Smith hoped that an "invisible hand" would guide the egoism of individuals for the maximum welfare of all. From a metaphysical perspective – Smith was a moral philosopher – he might well have meant the hand of God. This is what Smith experts assume.[3] Today, we know that the invisible hand does not exist. It is a pure hope, and neither economics nor economic policy operates on the basis of hopes. Markets do not automatically transform their participants' pursuit of self-interest into the common good. The constitutional mandate that "the use of property is also to serve the common good" falls short if there is no legal instrument like a common good balance sheet that documents how companies obey it. In fact, the probability that they violate the mandate is higher than that they comply, because in the global competition the decisive factor of survival is not to be "good" but to be "profitable". As long as financial gain remains the "bottom line" of business, Smith's dream is only a soap bubble. What happens in the real world if the utmost goal of human beings is to pursue their own advantage and to act against others is that they learn to take advantage of others and deem this to be right and normal. But if we take advantage of others we do not treat them as equals; we violate their dignity.

DIGNITY IS THE HIGHEST GOOD

When I ask students attending my lectures at the Vienna University of Economics and Business what they understand human dignity to be, I frequently encounter a general, awkward silence. The students do not appear to have heard or learned anything about it in the course of their studies. This is all the more alarming considering the fact that dignity is the highest value: it is the first-named value in countless constitutions and it forms the basis of the Universal Declaration of Human Rights.

Dignity signifies *value*: the *same, unconditional, unalienable* value of all human beings. Dignity requires no "achievement" other than existence. It is from the equal value of all human beings that our *equality* derives – in the sense that all human beings living in a democracy should have the same liberties, rights and opportunities. And only if everyone really does have the same liberties is the condition fulfilled for enabling everyone to be really *free*. Immanuel Kant wrote that human dignity can only be preserved in daily life and interactions if we deem and treat each other as being of equal value: "*So act that you use humanity, whether in your own person or in the person of any other, always at the same time as an end, never merely as a means.*" [emphasis Kant's][4] We may indeed derive advantages from dignified encounters as a *by-product;* according to Kant and common sense this happens automatically if everyone wants the best for all, builds up a foundation of trust, takes others seriously, listens to and esteems all others. But gaining an advantage should not be the *objective* of the encounter. By contrast, on the free market it is legal and customary to instrumentalize our fellow human beings, violating their dignity because our goal is not to protect it. Our goal is to gain personal advantage, and in many cases this can be achieved more easily if we take advantage of others and violate their dignity. What is decisive is my attitude and my priority: am I interested in the greatest good and the preservation of the dignity of all, which is something which affects me automatically and which I benefit from as well, or am I primarily interested in my own welfare and my own advantage, which others might, but will not necessarily draw benefit from?

If we pursue our own advantage as our supreme goal, the customary practice is to use others as means to achieve this goal and to take advantage of them accordingly. For this reason, Smith's perversion of goal and by-product leads to widespread violations of human dignity and the systematic restriction of the liberty of many.

A FREE MARKET?

The so-called free market would only be free if all its active participants could withdraw from any barter transaction without harm. But this is the case for only some of the transactions made on the market. In many cases, one party might find it harder to refrain from engaging in a particular transaction than the other because he or she depends on it to a higher degree.[5] Many people cannot decide whether to buy food on a certain day or not, whether to rent an apartment or not; many enterprises cannot decide whether to take out a loan on a certain day or not – if they do not, they might be bankrupt the next day; many farmers cannot decide freely if they want to deliver their goods or not – they often have only one or a handful of buyers to "choose" from, all of whom treat them equally poorly. For typical barter transactions the following applies:

- An average *employer* has an easier time terminating a work contract and is thus more able to determine the conditions of the work contract than the average employee is.
- An average *creditor* has an easier time terminating a credit agreement and is thus more able to determine the conditions of the agreement than the average borrower is.

- An average *landlord* has an easier time deciding not to sign a rent contract and is thus more able to determine the conditions of the rent contract than the average lessee is.
- An average *global corporation* has an easier time dispensing with one of its thousands of suppliers and is thus more able to determine the conditions of supply contracts than the average supplier is.

An imbalance in private barter relations would not matter so much if everyone were to treat each other with respect and the intention of preserving the other's dignity. Then the more powerful person would meet the less powerful at eye level, perceive them, take their needs and feelings as seriously as their own, and not be happy with the result until both found it acceptable. In market capitalism, however, the more powerful individual is outright encouraged to utilize their edge, and the imbalance of power, in the pursuit of their own advantage. The competition which results from this is what creates the particular "efficiency" of the free market.

If a human community does not systematically preserve the dignity of the individual then liberty will not be granted either, for the preservation of dignity – human beings treating each other as equals – is the precondition for liberty in every community. If all have an eye on their own advantage they do not treat others as equals any more but rather as "instruments", thus endangering the liberty of all. For this reason a market economy which is based on profit maximization and competition cannot be called a "free" economy; this would constitute an intrinsic contradiction.

TRUST IS MORE IMPORTANT THAN EFFICIENCY

If we must constantly fear that our fellow human beings will take advantage of us in the market as soon as they are in a position to do so, something else will be systematically destroyed: trust. Some economists say this doesn't matter because the economy focuses completely on efficiency. But such a view must be disputed, for trust is the highest social and cultural good we know. Trust is what holds societies together from the inside – not efficiency! Imagine a society in which you can trust every person completely – would that not be the society with the highest quality of life? And imagine the opposite, a society in which you had to mistrust everyone – would that not be the society with the lowest quality of life?

The interim conclusion to be drawn is radical: so long as a market economy is based on pursuit of profit and competition and the mutual exploitation that results from it, it is reconcilable with neither human dignity nor liberty. It systematically destroys societal trust in the hope that the efficiency it yields will surpass that achieved by any other form of economy. When such matters are pointed out to mainstream economists three familiar responses are commonly elicited:

1. There is no alternative to the market economy; this is common knowledge and thus all further discussion is unnecessary.
2. Whoever does not acknowledge this wants to catapult society back into poverty and the nineteenth century or drive it straight to communism, and we all know how that ended.
3. The market economy is the most productive form of economy there is; history has proved this. Competition spurs human beings to the highest levels of performance – this is in addition to the fact that it is rooted in human nature and is thus unavoidable.

We need to take a closer look at this last fundamental myth of the market economy: "Competition is in most cases the most efficient method we know," writes Nobel Prize laureate for economics Friedrich August von Hayek.[6] If a "Nobel Prize laureate" says this, it must be true – although there is no Nobel Prize for economics.[7] I have tried to find the empirical studies which led Hayek to this insight but I have found none. I explored other economists as well, for in the scientific community it is customary for colleagues to cite each other. And yet I found nothing here either. None of the economists who have won a Nobel Prize have ever proved through a study that "competition is the most efficient method we know". This cornerstone of economics is a mere claim which is believed by the large majority of economists. And capitalism and free enterprise, the world's dominant economic model for the past 250 years, is based on this belief.

Regarding the crucial question, does competition create stronger motivation than any other method? a plethora of studies have been conducted in numerous disciplines (educational science, social psychology, game theory, neurobiology) 369 of which studies were evaluated in a meta-study. And of those with a clear result an amazing majority of 87 percent found that competition is *not* the most efficient method we know;[8] cooperation is. The reason for this lies in the fact that cooperation motivates people *differently*. Competition motivates people too; no one contests this, and market capitalism has proved this, but it motivates them less. Cooperation motivates people through successful relationships, recognition, esteem, mutual goals and mutual achievements. This latter is the definition of cooperation. In contrast, the definition of competition is "mutually exclusive achievement of objectives". I can only be successful if someone else is unsuccessful. Competition primarily "motivates" people through fear. For this reason, fear is also a widespread phenomenon in market capitalism; many fear losing their job, their income, their status, their social recognition and place in the community. When people compete for scarce goods there are many losers, and most of them fear being affected themselves. And there is another component of motivation when it comes to competition. Aside from fear, competition elicits a form of delight – the delight in triumphing, in being better than someone else. And this is, when viewed from a psychological perspective, a very problematic motive, for the goal of our actions should not be to be better than the others but rather to perform our task well because we find purpose in it and do it gladly. This is what we should derive self-value from. Whoever derives self-value from being better than others is dependent upon others being worse. Psychologically speaking, this constitutes pathological narcissism: feeling better because others are worse is sick. The healthy thing to do would be to nourish our sense of self-worth by means of activities which we enjoy performing because we have chosen to do them of our own free will and see purpose in them. If we concentrated on being ourselves instead of being better, no one would be jeopardized and there would be no need for losers.

It is a matter of objectives. If I am better at performing a certain task than someone else but this is a *by-product* rather than my objective, then there is no problem. I will pay no attention to my being better and will not evaluate it as a "triumph" – and will help the other person. A problem ensues if my *objective* is to be better than someone else, if I am striving for a "win–lose situation" – which is the definition of competition used here. If my goal is to do my task well and I do not care how others do theirs, then I do not need any competition – but that is the very essence of the myth, namely that without competition human beings would have no incentive to perform, would not be motivated to do their tasks well. But according to psychological insights it is the other way around: motivation is stronger if it comes from within (one speaks of "intrinsic motivation") than if it comes from external sources ("extrinsic motivation"), for example from competition. The best performance is achieved not when there are competitors but rather when human beings are energized by devoting themselves to something and are utterly fulfilled by it. They do not need any competition for that.

If honest economists actually wanted to build the market economy on the basis of "the most efficient method" there is and they took notice of the current state of scientific research, they would have to base it on structural cooperation and intrinsic motivation. The fact that mainstream economists do not do this is an indication that science and insight play no role here but rather what dominates is the desire to underpin existing hegemonic structures ideologically. Those with power are served very well by competition: if we, as human beings, do not learn to cooperate and act in the spirit of solidarity we will not call power relations into question but rather will attempt, instead, to elbow our way into the realm of power and the social elite. In doing so, the majority will fall by the wayside. And the social climate will be poisoned to ever-increasing degrees because we will constantly take advantage of others, exploit and debase them in the pursuit of our own advantage, weakening and destroying trust and social bonds.

THE CONSEQUENCES OF THE PURSUIT OF PROFIT AND COMPETITION: THE TEN CRISES OF CAPITALISM

Contrary to the prognoses and promises held out by the theory of free enterprise, the pursuit of "self-interest" (Smith) as the supreme goal of competition leads to the following:

I. **The concentration and misuse of power.** The system-immanent pressure for growth – the pressure to become ever larger and more powerful and to ultimately obtain the status of a "global player" – leads to the emergence of gigantic corporations which misuse market power, close off markets, block innovation, and devour competitors or push them out of the market. In using such phrases as "brimming war chests", "hostile takeovers" or "kill your competitors",[9] the market idiom reveals what is ultimately at stake when it comes to the pursuit of one's own advantage.

2. **Suppression of competition and the building of cartels.** Once only a few players are left, adversarial conflict can suddenly turn into tactical, but not intrinsic cooperation. For the objective remains the same: maximum profit. If power allows the formation of cartels and oligopolies then preference will be given to this strategy because it is more effective than competition. Competition produces losers; cooperation produces only winners. This is why branch enterprises cooperate as soon as they can (this being inadvertent and unappealing proof of the superiority of cooperation – unappealing because in this case cooperation is not a goal but rather a means of achieving a wrong purpose, namely to take advantage of others). The recent bank bailouts show that the present economic model is not a matter of competition and free enterprise at all but rather of (governments) securing profits and power: this is the reason why the business and political elite cooperate and eliminate the competition – competition evidently not being the objective after all.

3. **Competition between locations.** States systematically try to attract enterprises and improve conditions for the pursuit of profit; the consequences are wage dumping, social dumping, fiscal dumping and environmental dumping, preferential treatment of global corporations over small local companies, and enticing special offers such as banking secrecy and removal of banking supervision because these are viewed as "locational advantages". If the egoism of enterprises infects states, nationalism will flourish in the midst of alleged "globalization".

4. **Inefficient pricing.** Prices are often not the rational result of the activities of rational market participants but rather the expression of power relations. The power created by supply and demand is often very unequally distributed, which is why prices often reflect the interests of the powerful rather than actual costs or values. The

care of children, sick persons, the elderly and gardens often is not rewarded financially at all, for example, whereas the maintenance of hedge funds is often astronomically expensive even though they have a negative impact on society.

5. **Social polarization and fear.** The market economy is a power economy. The larger – the more global – "free competition" is, the greater will be the imbalance of power between the protagonists, and with it the inequalities and the gap between the rich and the poor. In the USA the best-paid manager now earns 350,000 times the legal minimum wage.[10] This has nothing to do with "rational pricing" or with efficiency or justice: it is exclusively a matter of power. As a result, trust in society is declining and fear is rising. In the USA, trust among people has declined from 60 percent in 1960 to less than 40 percent in 2004.[11] The German Anxiety Index has risen from 24 percent in 1991 to 45 percent in the past few years.[12]

6. **Failure to satisfy basic needs and reduce hunger**. The explosion in the numbers of the famine-stricken shows how little globalized market capitalism is capable of satisfying even basic needs and thus protecting human rights. In the early 1990s hunger affected fewer than 800 million people, but in 2009, the Food and Agricultural Organization of the United Nations (FAO) reported that 1.023 billion were affected; between 2011 and 2013 the figure dropped to 843 million.[13] Satisfaction of basic needs is not the goal of capitalism; maximizing profit is. In many cases this leads to a situation in which basic needs that have no purchasing power are not met (with nutrition coming first, followed by medical care, housing and education), whereas purchasing power for which no need exists requires the "invention" of new needs (for example addictive foods, cosmetic surgery, SUVs). Capitalism systematically misdirects creativity and investments.

7. **Ecological destruction.** Since the supreme goal of capitalism is to increase financial capital (and not the common good), other goals such as environmental protection slide down the list of priorities. In its Millennium Synthesis Report the UNO ascertained that the health condition of almost all planetary ecosystems (oceans, fields, rivers, mountains, forests) deteriorated between 1950 and 2000. They are approaching their breaking point and sooner or later they will collapse. Then the "performance" of those ecosystems which are necessary to sustain human life will be in danger, impacting on climate stability, the regulation of humidity and temperature, the control of diseases and vermin, soil fertility and absorptive capacity. Capitalism is destructive because it strives blindly to increase financial capital rather than the natural foundations of human life and the economy.

8. **Loss of meaning.** Since the *objective* of capitalism is to accumulate material values, it quickly overshoots the *side effect* of satisfying basic material needs, subjugating all other values – quality of relationships and environment, time prosperity, creativity, autonomy – in the process. In the EU, working hours increased again by 8 percent between 1995 and 2005.[14] According to a poll conducted by Gallup, in the USA 70 percent of American employees are unengaged with their workplaces or even actively disengaged.[15] More and more people become increasingly alienated from their true desires and ideals and instead become addicted to consumption. With 24 million individuals affected, the compulsion to shop has become a pandemic in the USA.[16] In Austria, almost half of young people aged between 14 and 24 years are "significantly at risk of becoming shopping-addicted", with 10 percent "strongly endangered".[17] This is a kind of success in capitalist terms: the US economy invests more than $11 billion in its publicity attack on children.[18]

9. **Erosion of values.** In today's business world the most antisocial people make it to the top because what counts is optimization of monetary targets: people who are "more able" to filter out all other human, social and ecological goals are culturally "selected". Today egoists are particularly able to be "successful". If the business world systematically rewards egoism and competitive behaviour and people are viewed as successful if they work their way up in this dynamic of incentives, these values will rub off on all realms of society, starting with politics and the media and ultimately affecting our interpersonal relationships as well. As the German social psychologist Erich Fromm put it, "The capitalistic character shapes the societal character".[19]

10. **Shutdown of democracy.** When pursuit of profit and self-interest are the highest goals, business protagonists do their utmost to reach these goals. Not only interpersonal relationships, personal talents and natural resources are used as means to this end: needless to say, democracy is used as well. Since the times of Adam Smith the ethics of "self-interest" have placed this above the common good, the hope being that benefit to the common good will result as a by-product. The reality looks very different, however. Global enterprises, banks and investment funds become so powerful that they succeed in using lobbying, media ownership, political party financing and public–private partnerships to make parliaments and governments serve their particular interests rather than those of the common good. Thus democracy becomes the last and most prominent victim of "free markets".

I have published an extensive analysis of this elsewhere;[20] thus I will conclude these considerations here and begin to outline the alternative.

TWO
DEFINING THE ECONOMY FOR THE COMMON GOOD

All economic activity serves the common good.
Constitution of the Free State of Bavaria, Art. 151

THE GOAL OF ECONOMIC ACTIVITY

When I ask students at business schools and in university economics departments what the goal of economic activity is I almost always get the same answer: "Money!", "Monetary gain!", "Profit!" Then I ask, "Who says that?" "That's what we learn here," I am told. "And what sources do your teachers cite in telling you this?" Silence. "What is the justification for viewing gain or increase of profit as the goal of economic activity?" Silence.

I sought evidence of such notions in the constitutions of democratic states. To start with I looked for it in the constitution of Bavaria, Germany, where I read: "The entirety of economic activity shall serve the common wellbeing".[1] At first I thought this must be an error. But other constitutions claim the same thing: "Property entails responsibility" is what we read in Germany's Basic Law; "its use is

15

also to serve the welfare of the general public".[2] According to Italy's constitution "public and private economic activity should be oriented to the common good".[3] Colombia's constitution states: "Economic activity and private initiative are free within the limits of the common good."[4] The Constitution of Ireland says:

> We, the people of Eire (…) seeking (…) the common good (…) give to ourselves this Constitution // All powers of government (…) derive (…) from the people, whose right it is (…) to decide all questions of national policy, according to the requirements of the common good. // The State, accordingly, may (…) delimit by law the exercise of the said rights with a view to reconciling their exercise with the exigencies of the common good. // The State shall (…) direct its policy towards securing that the ownership and control of the material resources of the community may be so distributed amongst private individuals and the various classes as best to serve the common good.[5]

And the US constitution features in its preamble the words "promote the general welfare". The constitutions of democratic states are pervaded by a wide consensus as to what the goal of economic activity is: the advancement of the common good. In any case no constitution that I have read states that the goal of economic activity is to achieve monetary gain. Looking all the way back to ancient Greece, Aristotle called the focus on monetary gain "unnatural", distinguishing the "oikonomia" from the "chrematistike".[6] In the Western world there has been consensus for over two thousand years concerning the goal of economic activity. As you can see, the Economy for the Common Good is not suggesting anything new; it merely proposes that the constitutional goal of the economy should be implemented in the existing economic order as well.

PUTTING THE SYSTEM ON A NEW COURSE

To do this our current market economy would have to be put on a new course: directing our path away from pursuit of profit and competition, and instead striving towards pursuit of the common good and cooperation. The framework of legal incentives would have to abandon "maximization of self-interest" and embrace "the common good" as its guiding light instead, with the goal of all enterprise being to make the largest possible contribution to the common good. This is nothing new. The goals of individual economic protagonists would merely be harmonized with constitutional goals. This would be the first step towards an ethical reorientation of free markets.

REDEFINING ECONOMIC SUCCESS

Step number two: if the common good is the democratically defined goal then it would only be logical to measure economic success on the basis of whether or to what extent this goal is reached. And such success would have to be measured at all levels: at the level of national economies (the macro level), the level of individual enterprises (the meso level) and the level of every single investment (the micro level).

Today we measure economic success on the macro level in terms of gross domestic product, on the entrepreneurial level in terms of financial profit, and at the level of individual investment in terms of "return on investment" or "return on equity". What all three standard success indicators have in common is that they are "monetary" indicators. But money is not the goal of economic activity; it merely constitutes its means.

Now comes the crucial question: is it more meaningful to measure the success of projects in terms of the means they employ and the accumulation thereof or in terms of the goals they have and the extent to which these goals are reached? Perhaps this confusion of

17

goals and means is central to the problems of our current economic order. In our current system, methods of measuring success confuse goals and means. In capitalism, maximizing profit is the highest goal; promoting the common good may be used as a means of achieving this end but certainly not in all cases. In the Economy for the Common Good, improving the common good would be the highest goal, and capital would be a valuable means of attaining this. In some cases the accumulation of wealth could indeed be used to reach this goal, but in other cases it may not be necessary at all. Neither the use of money nor the increase thereof would be compulsory – the success of enterprises, investments and national economies would not be measured in terms of profit but rather in terms of the goal of promoting the common good.

The weakness of monetary indicators as parameters for measuring economic success is due to the fact that though money can best express the exchange value of a commodity – the value for which something is bought or sold – it has no use value by itself and is also incapable of expressing the use value of commodities and services. Yet the use value or usefulness of a commodity is of *primary interest* to human beings. It is the goal of economic activity. Exchange values can neither provide me with warmth nor nourish me. For that I need food, clothing, housing, relationships, intact ecosystems – in other words, use values. The GDP and financial gain provide no reliable information about the availability of use values. Does an increase in the GDP give any reliable indication, for example, of whether a given country:

- is free of hunger or homeless?
- is at war or in a state of peace?
- is a democracy or a dictatorship?
- is experiencing a decline or growth in the consumption of resources?

- has a just distribution?
- has equal rights for women or discriminates against them?
- has a society in which trust or fear is growing?

No matter which use value we consider, a rising GDP is not capable of measuring what really counts!

According to textbooks of economics the goal of economic activity is to satisfy human needs. They are the "ultimate end" of the entire enormous undertaking called "business". And if the most important needs of all human beings are satisfied then the famous vision of "prosperity for all" (Ludwig Erhard, former German Chancellor), the "general welfare" or simply the common good is achieved. So far, the slogan has been "The business of business is business". Our answer is: "The purpose of business is the common good."

MEASURE THE GOAL, NOT THE MEANS

The drawbacks of using GDP as an index of welfare have long ago been recognized, which is why the search for alternative indicators of prosperity began as early as the 1970s with Herman Daly's Index of Sustainable Human Welfare.[7] The London-based New Economics Foundation think tank created a Happy Planet Index.[8] The OECD developed the Better Life Index,[9] the Enquete Commission of the German Parliament on "Growth, Prosperity and Quality of life" defined the "W3" indicators,[10] and France's President Sarkozy created the Stiglitz–Sen–Fitoussi Commission to search for alternatives to the GDP.[11] The country which has made the most progress in this direction is the tiny nation of Bhutan with its "Gross National Happiness". No complex mathematical model was developed here; instead six thousand households are surveyed every two years, answering questions such as the following:

- How is your health?
- How well are you doing in comparison to the previous year?
- Will your children have a better life one day?
- Do you trust your neighbours?
- Do you get time every day to take a break/meditate/pray?

Many economists still claim that "happiness cannot be measured". And yet by assessing 33 indicators regarding all aspects of quality of life, as done in Bhutan, you can come much closer to what constitutes "happiness" than by using GDP as an index. In my opinion some twenty indicators would suffice to create the Common Good Product of any national economy. Developing such a thing could constitute a central project for the Common Good movement.

The Common Good Communities described below could be a start. In decentralized assemblies citizens could be asked to name the twenty indicators of life quality most relevant to them and from them derive a communal Life Quality or Common Good Index. Later, hundreds or thousands of such local indices for the Common Good Product at the domestic, the EU or even the international level could be synthesized.

We want to repeat this exercise on the level of business management. Does the amount of profit a company makes give us any reliable indication of whether:

- the company is creating jobs or downsizing;
- the working conditions are becoming more humane or more stressful;
- the company is mindful of the environment or exploits it;
- its income is distributed fairly;
- the company manufactures weapons or produces local organic foods?

The answer is clearly no. Financial profit gives us just as little reliable information about the development of even one use value, the satisfaction of even one basic need or the fulfilment of even one constitutional value. A rising GDP systematically fails to measure the goal of economic activity at all!

In the Economy for the Common Good the success of a national economy would be measured in terms of the Common Good Product; in a methodically sound manner and conforming to a large number of constitutions (the UK is a rare exception of a country without a constitution) the success of an enterprise would be measured in terms of its Common Good Balance Sheet. Today an enterprise can be "successful" while jobs are being cut, the environment is being destroyed, democracy is being undermined and meaningless products are being manufactured: in other words, a company can be viewed as successful even if it is contributing to the aggravation of every social and ecological problem. The automatic mechanism which Adam Smith believed in, namely that all would be cared for if everyone cared for him- or herself, does not exist. There *can* be a connection between profit and the common good but there is not *necessarily* any connection. The Common Good Balance Sheet would create a reliable connection: Adam Smith's hope of an invisible hand would be fulfilled by the creation of a visible hand, a method which measures and rewards the success of economic activity in terms of its contribution to society.

MEASURING THE COMMON GOOD

If the common good is the goal of all economic activity then it is only logical that this must be measured by a corresponding Common Good Balance Sheet, which would then become the main business balance sheet. What has hitherto served as the main type of balance sheet, namely the financial balance sheet, would become an auxiliary balance sheet. It would continue to represent how the enterprise covers its costs, investments and provisions and how it develops its financial resources, but it would not represent primary entrepreneurial "success". As in the past, enterprises that were striving to promote the common good would not want to make financial losses. Without profits, enterprises active in the market economy quickly fail. Profits should not be made for the sake of making profits, however. They are merely a means of fulfilling a purpose. What is currently experienced as "excessiveness", "exorbitance" and "greed" in capitalism would be eliminated if the use of profit was controlled by society to some degree. There will be more discussion on financial balance sheets later.

The Common Good Balance Sheet measures how key constitutional values which serve the common good are fulfilled by companies. As I have noted above, the five values "measured" by this balance sheet are nothing new. They are the most prevalent constitutional values of democratic states: human dignity, solidarity, justice, ecological sustainability and democracy.[16]

The Common Good Balance Sheet measures how these basic values are lived in regard to the stakeholders of an enterprise. Stakeholders constitute all groups of persons who are affected by the activities of an enterprise or who have a direct relationship to them: suppliers, investors, employees, customers, "competitors", local communities, future generations, and the environment. To make the Common Good Balance Sheet more transparent we have drawn up a Common Good Matrix in which the five basic values are entered on the horizontal x-axis and the stakeholders are entered on the vertical y-axis. At the intersections we currently measure seventeen Common Good indicators, for example:

- whether products/services satisfy human needs;
- how humane working conditions are;
- how environmentally friendly production processes are;

- how ethical sales activities are;
- how cooperative the enterprise's conduct is vis-à-vis other enterprises;
- how profits are distributed;
- whether or not women get equal treatment and equal pay;
- how democratic decision-making processes are.

What authority could "define" just what the common good means, however? There are answers to both questions. A plenitude of clearly defined and measurable indicators has already been elaborated by other corporate social responsibility standards and instruments ranging from the Global Reporting Initiative (GRI) and the SA8000 Social Standard to the OECD Corporate Governance Guidelines and the ISO environmental management systems.[12] All arrive at the same goals and values: How socially responsible is an enterprise's conduct? How ecologically sustainable are its production and distribution processes? How just is its distribution of profits? What is the quality of its workplaces? How is co-determination experienced? Does it support political responsibility (corporate citizenship)? The more clearly a democratic society focuses on defining such indicators, the more accurate and differentiated the results will be – just like physical measuring instruments become increasingly sophisticated once a sufficient number of people have honed and refined them.

The Matrix Development Team has developed seventeen indicators which are clearly measurable by assigning points. For each indicator, four levels can be reached: first steps, advanced, experienced and exemplary. In a handbook developed over the course of many years,[13] several pages are devoted to the description of each indicator, with information including the concept, the definition, the mode of measurement, examples and sources. The handbook is a work-in-progress document which – like all Economy for the Common Good documents – continues to be developed by a growing group of people in an open-source manner in the spirit of the creative commons.

DEFINING THE COMMON GOOD

And who "defines" the common good? Within the Common Good movement it is believed that this can only be done through a democratic process of discussion and decision making since the concrete meaning of the concept does not exist a priori and can change in the course of time. Historically speaking the concept dates back to Aristotle and his teacher Plato. It started to be applied precisely by Thomas Aquinas in the thirteenth century: "Bonum commune est melius quam bonum unius [The common good is better than the good of the one]"[14] Since then the concept of the common good has pervaded Christian social ethics as a "pole star".[15] But no matter how sublime the tradition might be, it could theoretically be postulated by a dictator or a totalitarian regime which claims to know best what is good for all. In fact both rightist and leftist dictatorships have employed the concept of the common good, but this is the unavoidable fate of all charismatic notions. "Freedom", "love" and "God" have certainly been hijacked and misused just as often – but this should not stop us from using these concepts; we simply have to define them democratically.

The model for the Economy for the Common Good requires a "definition" of the common good that is applicable to the instruments that measure success at three levels: investment, the enterprise and the national economy; the other economic-political measures do not require such a definition. The basic work needed to conceptualize the common good product can be done in common good communities. The Common Good Creditworthiness Assessment is currently being developed by the Bank for the Common Good in cooperation with other ethical banks. And the Common Good Balance Sheet is the core of the internationally growing Economy for the Common Good movement, which started in 2009 with a small circle of about fifteen businesspeople involved in the activist organization called Attac. The first version of the balance sheet, published in August 2010, was developed before the movement was founded. When the kick-off party for the Economy for the Common Good movement was given on 6 October 2010, this version was presented to the hundred or so attendees. In 2011, two dozen companies spontaneously agreed to do the balance sheet on a voluntary basis. With the help of an editorial staff of four, the preliminary concept was improved. At the request of the pioneering enterprises involved, the number of indicators was reduced from about fifty to seventeen with the aim of increasing its user-friendliness. Version 3.0 was the ultimately valid Common Good Balance Sheet for 2011; some 60 enterprises drew one up.

Common Good Balance Sheet versions 4.0 and 4.1 followed in 2012 and 2013. The editorial staff has grown with the movement, with one editor now in charge of each indicator. Each editor coordinates a team of experts and interested individuals and incorporates all feedback on the assigned criteria. So far, hundreds of individuals, enterprises and institutions have participated. In the years to come we anticipate that thousands and ultimately tens of thousands of enterprises, private individuals and organizations will contribute their experiences and expertise via the internet, at public events, and as pioneers. In this way the balance sheet will continue to be fine-tuned in the years to come.

This will not give it democratic legitimization, however. Once we deem it to be sound, that is, representative, precise and user-friendly, we could call for the election of an economic convention whose task would be to formulate a law, taking other preparatory work into consideration as well. Such a law would need to be agreed upon by the democratic sovereign (see page 00) and anchored in the constitution

Common Good Matrix 4.1

VALUE STAKEHOLDER	Human dignity	Cooperation and solidarity
A) Suppliers	A1: Ethical supply management	
B) Investors	B1: Ethical financial management	
C) Employees, including business owners	C1: Workplace quality and affirmative action 90	C2: Just distribution of labor 50
D) Customers/ Products/ Services/ Business Partners	D1: Ethical customer relations 50	D2: Cooperation with businesses in same field 70
E) Social Environment	E1: Value and social impact of products and services 90	E2: Contribution to the local community 40
Negative Criteria	Violation of ILO norms (international labor standards)/ human rights −200 Products detrimental to human dignity and human rights (e.g. landmines, nuclear power, GMOs) −200 Outsourcing to or cooperation with companies which violate human dignity −150	Hostile takeover −200 Blocking patents −100 Dumping prices −200

This is a simplified depiction. You can find the current version of the Common Good Matrix and the Common Good Balance Sheet at www.ecogood.org/

Ecological sustainability	Social justice	Democratic co-determination and transparency
		90
		30
C3: Promotion of environmentally friendly behavior of employees 30	C4: Just income distribution 60	C5: Corporate democracy and transparency 90
D3: Ecological design of products and services 90	D4: Socially oriented design of products and services 30	D5: Raising social and ecological standards 30
E3: Reduction of environmental impact 70	E4: Investing profits for the Common Good 60	E5: Social transparency and codetermination 30
Massive environmental pollution **−200**	Unequal pay for women and men **−200**	Non-disclosure of subsidiaries **−100**
Gross violation of environmental standards **−200**	Job cuts or moving jobs overseas despite having made a profit **−150**	Prohibition of a works council **−150**
Planned obsolescence (short lifespan of products) **−100**	Subsidiaries in tax havens **−200**	Non-disclosure of payments to lobbyists **−200**
	Equity yield rate > 10% **−200**	Excessive income inequality within a business **−150**

in the accepted form. A law or section of the constitution has rarely been drawn up so neatly. The Common Good Balance Sheet could be revised and newly adapted at any time. But such steps would always take over to avoid stack initiated and resolved by the sovereign people.

Let us return to the basic idea for a moment: a democratic society must be in a position to formulate the ten to thirty central expectations they have of enterprises, to demand accountability regarding them and to promote fulfilment thereof through the proposed incentive instrument. If it does not do this, the only alternative is to make sanctions and issue decrees, which is a more rigid form of regulation. The *currently used* mode of regulation is often not recognized as such. And yet "profit orientation", obligatory "financial reporting", "competition" (including cannibalism and "bankruptcies"), which result from all of this constitute an extremely effective regulatory order that incentivizes or even compels certain behaviours. The unfortunate results are widespread courses of action and strategies which harm society, destroy trust and damage relationships, but these are much too rarely ascribed to this misguiding legal framework, being all too often explained by flawed human nature instead. The Common Good Balance Sheet constitutes an attempt to correct this defective programming of the market and the "laws of the market", and to harmonize these laws with the values of relationships and (of) democratic societies.

DEMANDS MADE ON A UNIVERSAL BALANCE SHEET

The Common Good Balance Sheet would integrate itself into a growing spectrum of product labels (organic foods, Fair Trade), environmental management systems (EMAS, ISO), quality management systems (EFQM, Balanced Score Card), codes of conduct (OECD guidelines) and sustainability reports (GRI). The first generation of corporate social responsibility instruments proved to be generally ineffective, however. All standards are non-binding and no one is subject to legal monitoring. Unfortunately, the moment such standards start to conflict with the main balance sheet – the financial one – they are suddenly of no use anymore because this would attack the vital nerve, the famous "bottom line", of the enterprise and damage it in the framework of our current system dynamics. Whoever curbs financial gain for the benefit of a non-binding auxiliary balance sheet catapults him- or herself out of the race. This is also the reason why corporate groups insist that all such auxiliary balance sheets be non-binding in nature – because in this way they remain ineffective.

The Common Good Balance Sheet aspires to become the first corporate social responsibility instrument of the second generation which actually has an impact. The prerequisite for this is the fulfilment of eight essential requirements:

1. **Binding force.** The fact that doing things on a voluntary basis does not fulfil the goal has been proved by numerous corporate social responsibility instruments.

2. **A holistic approach.** It would not suffice to measure merely ecological aspects or the quality of workplaces: all basic values count!

3. **Measurability.** It should be possible to measure the results – that is, to evaluate them objectively.

4. **Comparability.** All enterprises should be accountable to the same goals/indicators; otherwise the more successful enterprises could not be rewarded.

5. **Comprehensibility.** Not only business consultants and Common Good auditors should understand the balance sheet but also customers, employees and interested members of the public.

6. **Publicity.** The Common Good Balance Sheet should be linked to a QR code and downloadable online.

7. **External audit.** This is to prevent enterprises from evaluating themselves – as is the practice for some corporate social responsibility instruments.

8. **Legal consequences.** Whoever contributes more to the community should be rewarded for this effort, following the principle of justice of performance.

The Common Good Balance Sheet meets all eight requirements, which is why it could have the desired effect of ethically rerouting the economy in the direction of sustainability, distributional justice and meaningful, health-promoting labour.

The Economy for the Common Good movement is striving to incorporate this approach into a current EU directive; in 2014 the EU Parliament issued a directive on "non-financial reporting".[16] It states that all enterprises with more than 500 employees are obliged to publish information which goes beyond key financial figures. In the first version of the directive, enterprises are offered a selection of various instruments, one of which they may, but don't have to use. The Economy for the Common Good movement is striving to see that these eight essential requirements are incorporated into the EU directive regardless of whether the future form of non-financial reporting is called an "ethics balance sheet" a "societal balance sheet" or a "common good balance sheet".

CREATE MARKET TRANSPARENCY

This is how the Common Good Balance Sheet works: depending on the degree to which targets are fulfilled the auditors assign a certain number of points for each balance sheet indicator. Every enterprise, whether it is run by a single person, a public charity, a utilities company, a medium-sized business or a market-listed joint-stock company, can reach a maximum of 1,000 Common Good points. To begin with, the results of the Common Good Balance Sheet could appear in the form of a label on all products and services, being colour-coded according to five categories, for example like this:

- negative score, Level 1, red.
- 0 to 250 points, Level 2, orange.
- 251 to 500 points, Level 3, yellow.
- 501 to 750 points, Level 4, light green.
- 751 to 1,000 points, Level 5, green.

This would enable consumers to get quick, concise information on the Common Good performance of the enterprise whose product they were thinking of buying. The Common Good colour could appear next to the barcode or the QR code of a product. If the customer scanned the code with his or her mobile phone, the entire Common Good Balance Sheet would appear on the display. It would be obligatory to make this accessible to the public. Consumers could immediately ascertain whether a product was "only" produced in an ecologically sustainable way and produced locally, or whether the company which made it also gave women equal pay for equal work and had a family-friendly working time model.

The "rationality" and "efficiency" of the market economy are justified in textbooks on the premise that all market participants have all information "completely" and "symmetrically" at their disposal. But this is not the case today; if we pull any product at random off the supermarket shelf it will not disclose who manufactured it, under what working conditions or with what environmental effects. Nor will it tell us whether women were treated the same as men in the process, whether the enterprise cooperated with its competitors or cannibalized them, whether it paid a fair amount of taxes or hid its profits in a tax haven, hired lobbyists or financed political parties. Measured in terms of its own theory, the market economy can be neither rational nor efficient because the prerequisite for this – transparent information – is lacking. It is not uncommon for advertising to give misinformation regarding the effect, content and origin of products. The Common Good Balance Sheet would bring the reality of the market economy closer to its theoretical ideal, thus making it more efficient.

REWARDING CONTRIBUTIONS TO THE COMMON GOOD

Now comes the decisive step: coupling the results of the Common Good Balance Sheet with differentiated legal treatment. The more Common Good points an enterprise obtained, the more legal privileges it would enjoy, almost in the conservative sense of "just desserts", for whoever does more for the community should be rewarded for it more by society. Suitable incentive instruments already exist; they would only need to be used systematically for performance aimed towards the Common Good, for example:

- a lower tax rate
- a lower customs tariff
- bank loans with better conditions
- preferential status for public procurement and the award of contracts (one fifth of the economic output!)
- research cooperation with public universities
- direct funding, etc.

Today, all enterprises are admitted to the market under the same conditions, irrespective of the degree to which they fulfil the values of the constitution or violate them and without any consideration of their ethical performance or lack thereof. The effect of this "equal treatment" is that the more ruthless and irresponsible protagonists on the market are more likely to win out because they are able to offer goods and services more cheaply. Those who act unethically are rewarded. This is the effect of the false "guiding light" of the economy.

In the Economy for the Common Good only "the same" would be treated equally; those who were "unequal" would be treated unequally, which is to say, higher performance would be rewarded. These legal advantages would help those who were oriented to the Common Good cover their higher costs. The consequence would be that ethical, sustainable and regional products manufactured and traded using fair methods would be less expensive than unethical, unsustainable, throwaway articles manufactured and traded using unfair methods. In this way ethical and responsible enterprises would systematically gain a stronger foothold on the market. The "laws of the market" would be harmonized with the basic values of society.

Should rewards turn out to be so generous as to enable an enterprise to make considerable profits, it would only be allowed to use these for certain purposes. There would be no use in maximizing profits for the benefit of self-interest. Benefit would be gained, however, through "maximization" of Common Good points: the better the Common Good Balance Sheet the higher the probability that an enterprise would survive. In contrast to the situation today, a company's financial balance sheet would no longer be the decisive factor when it came to surviving or not. An unethical company would be incapable of achieving a positive financial result.

The incentive effect could be reinforced: the Common Good Balance Sheet of an enterprise would improve to the degree that the Common Good Balance Sheet of the suppliers, subcontractors, credit institutions and other enterprises it cooperated with scored well. Through the interaction of consumer decisions, legal advantages, preferential status for "more successful" suppliers and subcontractors and money lenders, as well as Common Good audits by loan-granting banks, a powerful spiral of incentives with a bullwhip effect in the direction of the Common Good would ensue. Society would finally reach its goals in business.

COMMON GOOD AUDITS

A frequently asked question is: Who should audit the balance sheet? If companies were allowed to draw up a balance sheet themselves, then they could also evaluate it themselves. Would it not be necessary to create a Leviathan state which monitors and oversees enterprises every inch of the way?

The answer to this is no, there is – almost – no need for such a state. In this case the market would in fact regulate itself! To illustrate this point, let us start by looking at the procedure which is used for financial reporting today: a financial balance sheet is drawn up by the enterprise, audited internally and then sent out to a chartered accountant – a freelance professional. If the balance sheet is "verified" the state then comes along and demands taxes. The tax authority completes the process.

The procedure envisioned for the Common Good Balance Sheet is similar yet easier. The Common Good Balance Sheet would be drawn up by the enterprise (ideally with the participation of all employees) and audited internally (for example by a Common Good officer) and then externally, by the Common Good auditor. That is it. Once the Common Good auditor verified the balance sheet, the enterprise would automatically fall into a certain tax and customs tariff category and a certain class of credit terms. The state would do nothing except where public procurement and invitations to tender were concerned. Here the state would look at the Common Good Balance Sheet first, and then at the price.

In addition to legal accreditation and quality assurance for Common Good auditors, the state would only perform one other monitoring function – on a spot-check basis. In the event that an enterprise falsified its Common Good Balance Sheet, bribed the auditor or this person certified the falsified balance sheet, there would have to be a supervisory procedure and possibilities for sanctioning any corrupt auditors. But if there was the threat of a hefty fine for the first violation and withdrawal of the person's professional licence in the event of a second violation, auditors would consider carefully whether they should commit such a crime or not. For as opposed to financial balance sheets, Common Good Balance Sheets offers numerous advantages so far as the problem of fraudulent falsification is concerned:

- they are public and accessible to all;
- they are comprehensible to all because the criteria used are simple and humane;
- numerous stakeholder groups have a concrete interest in the accuracy of Common Good Balance Sheets; attempts at falsification would soon be revealed. Another aspect under discussion is "peer evaluation". All persons connected with an enterprise would participate in the evaluation in order to give auditors a broader basis of information for their work.

Enterprises would have an "intrinsic" interest in obtaining the highest possible number of Common Good points because of the prospect of certain advantages; nevertheless the implementation of each individual criterion would be "voluntary", which is why no state auditing official and no state bureaucracy (Ministry of the Common Good) would be required. The Common Good Balance Sheet controls the conduct of enterprises without setting off any additional regulatory orgy.

Analogous to the separation of consultation and inspection in the case of financial balance sheets, these services should be separated for Common Good audits as well. A legal body would probably be required for certifying Common Good auditors so as to ensure the quality of their work. It might be the same as for financial auditors.

In light of the complexity of the subject, it is also conceivable that audit teams would be needed instead of individual auditors. This would also serve to improve inspection results and more effectively safeguard the process against bribes.

PROFIT AS MEANS

So much for the Common Good Balance Sheet. But what would happen to the financial balance sheet? First of all: it would continue to be drawn up by all companies, especially since the Economy for the Common Good would constitute a form of market economy (but a cooperative and ethical rather than a capitalistic one) in which private enterprises, money and market-generated product prices would exist – albeit under different conditions and prerequisites than today's. But since financial gain would no longer be the goal, the financial balance sheet would become an auxiliary, or rather, a means balance sheet – entirely analogous to money, but which should actually only constitute a means of exchange and not the purpose thereof. The purpose of exchange is to satisfy needs. Financial balance sheets fulfil a key condition for this but they are not the actual object of entrepreneurial activity. The purpose of entrepreneurial pursuit, its societal task, is represented by the Common Good Balance Sheet. The purpose of financial gain would be inverted; it would become the means rather than the goal.

Just what does this mean? We have worked hard to hone this crucial aspect of the Economy for the Common Good. Since profits can either be beneficial or detrimental to an enterprise – either increase or reduce the common good – their use would be differentiated according to this very criterion. Uses of financial profit which reduced the common good would be restricted. This way the "excessive nature" of capitalism – accumulation for the sake of accumulation – would be channelled in a meaningful direction. Use of financial gain for the purpose of hostile takeovers, demonstrations of power, exploitation, destruction of the environment and crises would have to be halted altogether, whereas financial excess used to create added social and ecological value and for making investments and engaging in cooperation – in short, to increase the common good – would be endorsed and even promoted. Such distinctions are made everywhere. I may use a knife to cut vegetables but not to slay human beings. Laws regulate permissible and forbidden use of tools and the conditions and limits put on the use of tools and weapons. It should be the same with profits made by enterprises because in the Economy for the Common Good such tools – like money in general – would constitute exactly that: mere tools, not the goal in and of itself. Otherwise they could become lethal weapons.

PERMISSIBLE USES OF PROFITS

I. Investments

A large proportion of national economic investments is financed by the financial surplus, that is, the profits of enterprises. This may and should stay the same in the future, for investments can have a beneficial effect which increases the common good and enhances quality of life. It is necessary to differentiate clearly between tools and goals, however, because like a kitchen knife, investments can be used in different ways, for example to (a) generate renewable forms of energy, produce bio-organic foods and offer educational and healthcare services or to (b) slash and burn rainforests, start up a mass livestock farm, manufacture gas-guzzling SUVs or make nuclear weapons. Thus in the future such investments should only be made which generate an added social or ecological value. To achieve this – analogous to financial cost calculations customarily made today – a Common Good calculation would have to be made for every considerable-sized investment. This way an additional instrument of the Common Good – in addition to the one which measures enterprises' overall performance – would have an advance effect on investment decisions. This would prevent inhumane production conditions from being created, environmental damage from being incurred and high-risk technologies from being developed in the first place. The structural core of this idea entered the political arena long ago; various circles of society have proposed social impact, sustainability and non-discrimination assessments and so forth. This should also be applied to investment decisions made by companies, for just as laws determine the direction in which a democratic community develops, investment decisions determine the direction which enterprises and the national economy take. Such decisions should be made as circumspectly as possible, and they should definitely be based on a more complex foundation of assessment than mere financial profitability, which is almost the only factor taken into consideration when decisions are made today. For borrowing of outside capital, an external audit conducted by a bank would be necessary in addition to an internal Common Good audit of the planned investment. The Democratic Bank, which has already started to take shape since the first edition of this book, in the form of the Projekt Bank für Gemeinwohl (Project Bank for Common Good), would not only assess the financial standing of the credit applicant but also the added value for the Common Good. Business plans of the future would look very different from how they look today.

2. Reserve assets

In a money market economy, no enterprise can end the business year without making either gains or losses. Sometimes business goes better, sometimes worse. That is why two tools – loss carryforward (used for balancing and tax declarations) and reserves for future losses – exist. Both instruments should be used in the future as well so as to give enterprises a certain amount of leeway. Reserves should be dependent upon two decisive conditions, however. First of all, they should be restricted (for example to five years and a small percentage of the turnover). Second, it should not be permissible to use them for financial investments. Should they exist in the form of liquid assets it should be required that they be deposited in a bank with a Common Good orientation such as the Democratic Bank to prevent them from being withdrawn from the money supply.

3. Increase of capital

The third permissible use of financial surplus would be the paying back of borrowed funds, that is, bank loans. A look at average equity quotas allows us to presume that this use of financial surplus would not bring about any great change of the current situation. Most enterprises are indebted to quite or extremely high degrees, and the profits they make are not high enough to pay back their debts. For such enterprises nothing much would change. In the Economy for the Common Good, however, the indebtedness of enterprises would lose two of its negative aspects. The Common Good assessment of all loans would prevent destructive investments from being financed and smoothen the pressure on the economy to grow because of interest since it would be replaced by fixed-rate fees just large enough to cover the operating and resilience costs of the bank involved.

4. Dividend payouts to employees

If a year ended more successfully than anticipated, all of those who contributed to this success can be rewarded financially. Incomes would be limited to a certain multiple of the statutory minimum wage, however – and this would apply to employed proprietors as well. Just how high the limit should be would be worked out by the economic convention and the democratic sovereign.

5. Loans to other enterprises
Anyone wanting to help other enterprises, customers and suppliers could grant them interest-free loans. Since cooperation would be promoted systematically, this form of direct (financial) solidarity would be promoted as well. This would make cash transactions cheaper and enterprises would save themselves the trouble of going to a bank and paying fees or interest.

NON-PERMISSIBLE USES OF PROFITS

All of the above has been permitted in the past. What is decisive is the list uses that would no longer be permissible:

I. Financial investments
Enterprises should earn their income exclusively from the products they manufacture and/or the services they provide, not from financial operations. A hairdresser is there to cut hair or do cosmetic treatments and not to make money from money; a farm exists to produce healthy food and keep the agrarian ecosystem stable and diverse, not to make money from money. A bank should be there to convert saved money into reasonably priced loans, not to make money from money. Today corporations have stopped being net debtors and turned into net creditors because they no longer earn their income with production alone but rather with casino bets, stock trading and interest-rate business. Many industrial corporations are referred to as "large banks with a small workbench"; the pharmaceutical giant Roche has been called "a large bank with a small pharmacy attached to it".[17] In the Economy for

the Common Good, money would only be a means for production, no longer a means of making profit (Aristotle's 'chrematistics'). Financial casinos would be a thing of the past. Financial assets except those stored in the company safe would be deposited in non-profit-oriented banks so that money could be put at the service of the common good and passed on quickly and inexpensively to those currently in need of it as a resource. In the Economy for the Common Good, money would always also constitute a part of public infrastructures and not only private assets. It would be a public good.[18]

2. Dividend payouts to proprietors who do not work in the enterprise

The core of capitalism is that some people – owners of capital, those with power – appropriate the added value of work done by others – non-owners of capital, the powerless ones – and they do so legally. This is what Marx taught us in detail. The question is how it has happened that so few own so much capital and so many so little, and what can be done about it in systemic terms. The tricky thing about the debate is that there are many different ways to acquire a large amount of capital. Some of them are reconcilable with all the basic values of society (personal effort coupled with consideration of others and the bearing of responsibility), whereas others contradict such values to the extreme (ruthless greed and lust for power, trickery, luck or the inheritance of large fortunes made without the inheritors ever lifting a finger). The possibility of paying out dividends on company earnings to people who have not participated in the value-adding work process often fails to promote personal engagement and responsibility, fostering dangerous tendencies instead:

- **The decoupling of power and responsibility.** Through the separation of the proprietors of an enterprise who make the

decisions and the employees who work there, such free rein
is given to irresponsibility that this encourages unscrupulous
behavior. Profitable sites are closed down, thousands of jobs are
destroyed, and long-term investments are neglected, for example.

- **Unjust distribution to the point of exploitation.** Anonymity
  fosters disproportion and excess. In recent years, the rates of profit
  in many countries rose while wages stagnated. In 2010, seven of
  the thirty corporations listed at the Frankfurt stock market paid
  out more money to stockholders than the sum of the previous
  year's profits. We are making a transition from dividends to
  expropriation. At the same time large corporations pay less and
  less tax and even receive tax credits.
- **Meaningless motives.** Profit can be a motive for founding a
  company in which the founder takes no personal or creative
  interest.
- **Concentration of power.** If I may own a company that I do not
  work in, I can own hundreds of companies and that makes me
  richer and more powerful all the time (and the assets and the
  increase in power which come with them become the goal, not
  the purpose). Inequitable distribution of property by enterprises is
  a key source of inequality in terms of income as well as assets.

It would be more responsible and more just in terms of performance
to make work the sole source of income and to keep decision-making
power primarily in the enterprise, and for this reason:

1. Capital should be only a means; its increase should not be the
   purpose of running or founding an enterprise;
2. This means should be distributed more equitably than today, in
   particular at the "start", that is, the beginning of an individual's
   working life ("equal opportunities");

3. Acquisition of capital should be coupled fundamentally with personal performance and responsibility;
4. Return on investment should benefit those who contributed to it through their work.

For this reason only those persons who work in a company should receive income from company earnings. In the Economy for the Common Good there would be a statutory maximum and minimum wage for every work hour. The maximum wage could be seven, ten, twelve or twenty times the minimum wage, for example. Whoever worked longer hours would be allowed to earn more but for every individual hour – apart from special or night shifts – there would be a defined maximum spread. The maximum spread would be defined democratically – by the sovereign people.

The main purpose of limits on dividend payouts is to dry up a key source of inequality and the concentration of power. If capital can be "poured out" of enterprises, as the word for dividend payout in German ("Ausschüttung") suggests, then the "incentive" for owners to do this against the interests of the enterprise and of the people who work there grows. A select few make decisions and harvest the fruits without even working in the company themselves.

For the vast majority of enterprises, nothing would change through this because they do not pay out dividends to persons outside the company. A misunderstanding frequently arises here: today many small businesses look upon themselves as "profit-oriented" and interpret the income they derive from operating surplus as "profit" which is as such their own income. This may and should stay that way in the future – the difference being, however, that such income would be viewed as payment for people who work in the company: as pay for the entrepreneur. (The aforementioned problem is not that dividends are paid out to entrepreneurs who engage in the work of the company but rather that they are paid to persons who do *not*.) The large majority of business partnerships would generate such little "profit" that the entrepreneur's income would lie well below the stipulated maximum multiple of the statutory minimum wage. Such persons would not be affected by "limitation of profit" at all.

Those affected most would be joint-stock companies. For the aforementioned reasons no dividends should exist in the future. Several factors regarding joint-stock companies are not very well-known: (a) stocks contribute less and less to the financing of enterprises: in the USA the stock market sucked more money out of joint-stock companies than it pumped into them for the entire course of the 1990s; in France the balance was zero;[19] (b) innovative start-ups rarely get stock capital; usually relatives are the ones who help out;[20] (c) in many joint-stock companies the connection between property and responsibility has vanished.

Joint-stock companies were originally set up as special risk enterprises. The owners were liable and had to put their entire assets at the disposal of the company as a form of security. In 1856, the USA decided to limit personal liability to the measure of an entrepreneur's financial participation in his or her enterprise.[21] Today more and more taxpayers are liable for shareholders when ailing banks and automobile manufacturers need to be rescued, for example. These owners, instead of being obliged to inject additional capital into their staggering companies, are in fact rewarded by the taxpayers for their poor economic performance and their lack of responsibility. This promotes the tendencies of joint-stock companies to act irresponsibly and ruthlessly and to undermine democracy.

A frequently asked question regarding this issue is why people would put their savings at the disposal of a company if they cannot obtain any financial return on investment any more. Who should take the risk of the credit grantors upon themselves? Here is a systematic answer to this question: in the Economy for the Common Good, enterprises would be able to acquire (financial) capital "externally" in four different ways:

1. **Outside funding from Common Good-oriented banks.** Since banks would not pay out dividends or pay interest on savings, loans would be less expensive on average because the credit fees would only need to cover the operating costs of the bank. Moreover, the global financial casino would be closed, and for this reason people's assets would pile up at the banks and be available in large quantities.

2. **Equity.** People could participate in businesses. The difference would be that they would not receive any *financial* return on interest for doing so, nor would they be able to sell their share on markets (stock markets). They would have three advantages, however: (1) Meaning: they would help create a purposeful enterprise. (2) Values: they would only invest in companies with an excellent common good balance sheet. (3) Co-determination: for their equity they would receive a (per capita) say in a company and help shape it as they saw fit. Besides these three wins, they would get their money back if they needed it – after all, it was not a gift. Since from the perspective of the company it would constitute cost-free capital (because no interest would have to be paid on it), and hence be cheaper than a bank loan, the company would have a large incentive to attract equity. In return, they would have to become very appealing to investors. Since the magnet would no longer be money, it would have to be something different: a social purpose and ethical values! The most socially purposeful and ethically driven enterprises would acquire enough capital, and the instrument that would help them do this would be the Common Good Balance Sheet. All of a sudden the entire system would be running in the right direction.

Since financial assets would increase constantly in proportion to the economy, a growing part of private financial wealth would have to embark on a "quest for meaning". In other words, it would suffice to put a part of one's private financial assets at the disposal of an enterprise free of charge because there would be increasing amounts of financial assets.

3. **Equity from endowments.** This would be supplied by young employees who contributed their "democratic dowry" to the enterprise, increasing its equity in this way. The reform of inheritance law (Chapter 4) would make it possible for young people to contribute not only their working power but also a certain measure of capital to the company.

4. **Cost-free external funding.** Enterprises could give each other interest-free loans. They would be rewarded for doing so. Those who had more than they needed would not receive interest from the bank any more. Their profit would be the experience of solidarity and improvement of their Common Good Balance Sheet.

In the Economy for the Common Good, money would play a different role than it does today. As a means of exchange and equity for one's own company it would remain a predominantly private good, but as credit or capital for other companies it would tend to become a public good.

3. Hostile takeovers and mergers

The third non-permissible use of financial surplus would be buyouts of other enterprises against their will. Through the new orientation of enterprises the most frequent motive for hostile takeovers would disappear; if enterprises are no longer profit-oriented, they quickly and almost automatically abandon growth orientation *as their goal.*

It would no longer be necessary to grow as large as possible in order to (a) obtain higher profits, (b) devour a competitor and (c) keep from being devoured by a competitor.

Generally speaking, there would be no more monetary growth goal in business since growth would only constitute a means towards a new goal, this being to make the largest possible contribution to the common good as measured by the new economic success indicators. Should investments, increases in returns or friendly mergers serve this goal, then they would be welcome. In the event of a planned merger, a yet-to-be-defined majority of the employees, managers and owners of the two companies involved would have to approve it, however. This would put an end to hostile takeovers which – in the dictatorship of those with the most capital – are common practice today.

4. Party donations
It would be forbidden for enterprises to finance political parties or members of parliaments. Only individuals would be allowed to do so – perhaps up to a maximum amount.

Conversely, corporate property tax could be eliminated. The state should have no interest in *high* profits and should not participate in the pursuit of profit as a *goal* either. And taxing a means which brings benefits does not really make sense anyway. Or, alternatively, the corporate profit tax could be scaled according to the common good balance sheet result.

THE END OF THE COMPULSION TO GROWTH

This reorientation of financial profits would be used to redirect the entrepreneurial pursuit of success. Profit maximization would be neither desirable nor in fact achievable. There would be no "profit distribution" any more; for incomes there would be lower and upper limits, hostile takeovers would be forbidden and success would be measured in terms of the Common Good Balance Sheet.

Through the sum of these measures the growth compulsion in business would be eliminated, as such a compulsion results from the combination of "measuring success with a monetary indicator" (= pursuit of financial profit) and competition. If I compete with other enterprises, my profit margin must be higher than theirs because otherwise my rating will be worse, my financing costs will increase and I will be devoured in no time. Just how decisive financial profit is for the survival of a company is often underestimated. The success of an enterprise is determined by a plenitude of influential *factors* such as quality, innovation, efficiency, ethics, scrupulousness, size, flexibility … But there is only one single decisive *condition*: financial profit. At the end of the day financial profit determines the success or failure of a company, irrespective of quality, innovative force, size, marketing, social responsibility and all other factors.

And growth serves to yield higher profits than the competitors do, to ward off hostile takeovers, or to devour others. Growth is intrinsic to the system if it is programmed for pursuit of profit and competition.

Hence the reprogramming. If success were no longer equated with financial profit and companies were not allowed to devour each other, enterprises could finally find out what size is "optimal" and purposeful for them in a composed, anxiety-free fashion and then strive to reach it. The capitalistic system dynamics would disappear and everyone would be liberated from the general compulsion to grow and devour each other!

OPTIMAL SIZE

"Anyone who believes exponential growth can go on forever in a finite world is either a madman or an economist, "This is how the award-winning US economist Kenneth Boulding puts it.[22] For many of his colleagues this view remains inacceptable: "One must put things right: sustainable development is synonymous with the greatest possible long-term economic growth"; this is the claim made by the former Dean of Political Economics at Vienna University of Economics, Erich Streissler.[23] What I deem to be the most valuable insight on the topic of growth comes from the political scientist Leopold Kohr, who observes that in nature growth is a means of reaching the optimal size.[24] This is exactly what the focus should be on in business: enterprises striving to reach the optimal size. Today growth is a goal in and of itself, but tomorrow it would merely be a means. If something is too small, it is fine for it to get larger. If an enterprise has become hypertrophic, however, like a bank "too big to fail", then the optimal change in size is negative. In the Economy for the Common Good negative growth would be no problem as long as use values – values of the common good – grow. In the currently dominant economic order this would constitute a huge disaster, however, for shrinking is synonymous with recession and depression.

The human organism – like those of all other living creatures – illustrates well the role which growth could meaningfully play: up to an "optimal size" we grow materially. From a certain point on, this type of growth ceases. Then development shifts to the non-material dimensions: to emotional, social, intellectual and spiritual maturation. Human beings are not less "successful" because they do not keep growing physically throughout their lifetime. And they are not less happy either.

STRUCTURAL COOPERATION

The mental exercise posed by the Economy for the Common Good which is perhaps the most difficult to perform is the paradigm shift from competition to cooperation, which is to say that enterprises would no longer need to act in opposition to one another and would be rewarded for refraining from doing so.

Some readers will certainly have a hard time digesting this because today it is looked upon as "normal" for competitors to seek to damage or even liquidate each other. Thus it would actually be more fitting to speak of "counter-petition", because "competition" comes from the Latin words *cum* (together) and *petere* (search), which would actually be a much more apt equivalent of the word "cooperation". It stands for the common search – of market participants – for the best solution for all. Is it not self-evident that "searching against each other" cannot be efficient? Group intelligence is higher than anyone's individual intelligence. Almost all great technical developments derive from the contributions of many, not merely that of a single human being. Scientific advance is the result of the cooperation of countless researchers and thinkers over the course of history.

In the Economy for the Common Good, competition would not be eliminated. The Economy for the Common Good would be a form of market economy and as such would be based on some of its present foundations: private enterprises (= market) and money as means of exchange. As long as there is a right to found enterprises and the possibility of going bankrupt there will always inevitably be the *possibility of* "counter-petition". If it is promoted and stoked, the economy becomes a battlefield. If on the other hand it is placed at a disadvantage by a legal framework of incentives, it can become almost invisible within the primary structure of cooperation.

Thus in the Economy for the Common Good competition would be possible. (Theoretically competition would even be possible in an economy based completely on solidarity: the cooperatives might violate their ethos and start to compete with each other. This is due to the fact that everyone would have the same freedom to found a cooperative.) But the more businesses there were that stuck their elbows out, the more aggressively they acted *against* each other, the poorer their Common

Good Balance Sheets would become as a result. The more cooperative their conduct was and the more helpful they were to each other, the better the result of their Common Good Balance Sheet would be and the greater the probability would be that they would survive – not at the cost of others but rather to their benefit. The current win–lose order would be replaced by a win–win order.

How can enterprises help each other? As with neighbours and friends, there are many different ways, for example:

- by sharing their knowledge according to the open-source principle and with the help of creative commons licences;
- by helping each other out with labour;
- by passing on contracts;
- by providing cost-free loans and liquidity equalization.

They can also help each other by doing away with hostile opposition, for example by refraining from:

- advertising in mass media (setting up transparent-egalitarian product information systems instead);
- using dumping prices to conquer and secure markets;
- using blocking patents;
- devouring each other.

If enterprises were rewarded for mutual aid, then structural opposition and the currently practised destructive competition and cannibalism would turn into peaceful coexistence at least, and in the best case (thanks to legal incentives) be replaced by active cooperation. Whoever thinks this is an invitation to cartelization continues to subscribe to the capitalistic logic of today. Today cartels are not ends in themselves but rather means of increasing profits. If profits were limited and used to increase the common good, then cartelization as a means would lose all its meaning. Cooperation, on the other hand, is an efficient means of fulfilling the aim of entrepreneurialism more successfully. Suddenly cooperation would no longer contradict the ultimate goal of business, but rather harmonize with it.

Pursuit of optimal size and thus abandonment of growth as a goal in itself would increase the willingness of many enterprises to engage in cooperation. This is because an enterprise which has reached its optimal size has a much easier time divulging its know-how and passing on contracts. From evolution we have learned that (a) more and more species are evolving, and (b) the individual specimens of the species that exist do not always get bigger. The Harvard mathematician and biologist Martin Nowak writes: "Cooperation is the chief architect of evolution."[25]

BANKRUPTCY

A third aspect of the Economy for the Common Good – in addition to money and private (productive) equity – which indicates that it constitutes a form of market economy is the possibility of bankruptcy. But in comparison to capitalistic economies based on competition, bankruptcy would be less probable because:

1. the tendency would be for only enterprises with a higher purpose to be founded since profit as a motive for founding enterprises would disappear;
2. in democratic enterprises employees would tend to pull together and, through mutual ways of handling things, bankruptcy could be prevented more effectively;
3. third, and most important, enterprises would cooperate more and compete less (they would be rewarded for this, not be compelled to do so).

Enterprises that refused to engage in cooperation or only met minimum statutory standards would tend to have poorer prospects for success. Such enterprises would face the largest threat of bankruptcy. Due to their poor Common Good Balance Sheet score they would fail to win the trust of the consumers and investors and also lose out on legal advantages, incurring relatively severe disadvantages compared to other enterprises that were capable of cooperating and taking responsibility instead. The situation would be exactly the opposite of what it is today, with unscrupulous wage squeezers, polluters and tax evaders gaining cost benefits and thus also competitiveness. Today, power and size often win out over quality – and values.

COOPERATIVE MARKET REGULATION

The Economy for the Common Good is a market economy, not a centrally planned one. If implemented, there would be market fluctuations in the future as well. It could happen that the demand in a certain sector suddenly nosedived or the supply soared due to the market entry of new enterprises. (Increases in demand and drops in supply would presumably pose no big problem for enterprises.) What would happen in the Economy for the Common Good if there were a need for fewer enterprises or at least fewer work hours due to declines in demand or technological innovation?

Let's begin by looking at what the classic reaction would be today: the increasingly "tough" competition would get tougher and tougher and all the competitors would try to undercut each other's prices until one or several of them – in the worst case all simultaneously – gave up, declared bankruptcy or were taken over. Today's market competition is a win–lose economic order.

In the Economy for the Common Good all enterprises in the affected sectors that were willing to cooperate could convene a "crisis or cooperation commission" and mutually discuss whether it would benefit the common good best if they:

1. reduced all work hours proportionally;
2. cut workplaces proportionally and organized retraining measures;
3. downsized one enterprise considerably or made joint efforts to equip it for a new task;
4. closed down an enterprise and found alternative workplaces for those affected;
5. facilitated the voluntary merger of two enterprises into a smaller overall unit – on condition that this enterprise was not too large (this to be judged according to "objective" = societal/legal criteria as well as "subjective" = democratic criteria).

Or they could find other ways to deal with the situation. It would be advisable for the regional economic parliament to participate in finding systemic solutions. If labour were urgently needed in other sectors, retraining measures could be organized.

Even if all options were exhausted, one could not always prevent some enterprises from being eliminated. In the Economy for the Common Good, projects too might fail; room for "risk" – and freedom – would remain. But whereas today the enterprise with the poorest financial results would be eliminated – irrespective of quality, ecological mindfulness and social responsibility – in the Economy for the Common Good the enterprise with the poorest Common Good Balance Sheet would have to go – the one that had been unwilling to do something for the community, to cooperate with others or to let itself be helped by others.

The decisive difference from today would be that enterprises would proceed in a solidarity-minded way and attempt to keep everyone in the boat – whereas it is currently permissible to throw others overboard or devour them.

THE COMMON GOOD AND GLOBALIZATION

Many of those who attend my lectures are worried that ethical enterprises would immediately be swept off the market by global competition, arguing that "the entire world" would have to participate to make the Economy for the Common Good work. This perspective is proof of the successful indoctrination of ideologists and of those who profit from the current economic order, which they depict as "natural" or "without any alternative", while failing to recognize the political roots of such unfair (site-related) competition, "free trade" and free movement of capital. In a free trade regime the most ethical enterprises do indeed lose out; this is exactly the error of this system. Good conduct and loyalty to the constitution are punished. "Free trade" favours enterprises that disregard and violate the laws and values achieved in the EU (member states) democratically rather than those enterprises that venerate and observe such laws and values. If both kinds of enterprises are admitted to the market under identical conditions there is no question which will win out. Free trade is a political invitation to site relocations and the export of workplaces. How low must the self-esteem of a democratic commonwealth be which undermines its own rules and regulations by making free trade agreements with countries which have no such regulations themselves? Free trade violates the constitution!

I see two possible solutions. The first would be a global regulatory approach. A mutual framework – standards for labour practices, social affairs, consumer protection, the environment, taxation and transparency – would have to be in place before economic liberties were granted. For this approach the United Nations, as the heart of international law, would be the best regulating body.

Concrete implementation could look like this: a UN member state would grant all countries free trade which fulfilled the UN Civil and Social Pacts (both human rights conventions), the International

Labour Organization labour standards, the multilateral environmental agreements including the Climate Convention, the UNESCO Convention for the Protection of Cultural Diversity and the (future) agreement on automatic information exchange of fiscal data. For each agreement that has not been ratified, there would be an extra tariff, for instance:

UN Civil Pact	+ 20% tariff
UN Social Pact	+ 20% tariff
UN Climate Convention	+ 20% tariff
Other UN environmental agreement	+ 10% tariff
Single ILO core labour standard	+ 5% tariff
UNESCO Convention	+ 10% tariff
Automatic information exchange of fiscal data	+ 20% tariff

The second approach would be an incentive-based Economy for the Common Good, which would obligate all enterprises to draw up a Common Good Balance Sheet. The better the result, the "fairer" the trade, the "freer" market access would be. Free trade would be a privilege of the fairest enterprises. The less fair or ethical an enterprise was, the higher the ethical protective duty would be. This would put an end to unfair competition and location competition. The greatest advantage of the second approach would be that the EU would not need to wait for an agreement to be drawn up by the UN; instead, as the largest and most powerful economic area in the world, it could easily venture going it alone. The best solution would be a parallel strategy combining the two approaches: while protecting the domestic market through a differentiated customs regime, the EU would urge for fair and binding trade regulations in the framework of the UNO. This would not even be a new approach. After all, the EU was the body that pushed through the free trade conditions currently in effect – the those that violate human rights, hamper development and ignore the need for sustainability. Thus the prerequisite for the vision put forth here would be radical democratization of the EU.

So long as there were countries which did not go along with this, the EU could begin with a group of pioneer nations: with a Common Good Zone. This would be a fair-trade zone which agreed on mutual social, ecological and taxation regulations. And which protected itself from countries in which such regulations did not exist. This would be a completely legitimate form of protection – of protecting the constitution!

SOCIAL SECURITY AND WORK LEAVES

So long as the possibility of bankruptcy remains, it can happen that human beings lose their place of gainful employment and thus their source of income. This is one of the reasons why, in an Economy for the Common Good, all people would take off one year for every decade of employment and find fulfilment in other ways during that time. For a person who spent forty years of his or her life working that would amount to four free years. This would – if everybody participated – reduce the pressure on the job market by about 10 percent, and the current unemployment in the EU would be eliminated altogether. Those taking time out would be "on leave". During this time they could receive, for example, 80 percent of the average income of the past five working years or income set in some other democratic way. By allowing all human beings to take such a "work leave", envy would no longer be an issue; everyone would have equal rights and no one would have to finance the others. This life opportunity would not only elevate the self-esteem of many human beings who are currently unemployed but also increase the general feeling of freedom, for these years could be used to train for new skills, devote oneself to one's family, engage in art, find leisure, enjoy nature or embrace other passions. The status of productive labour and gainful employment would be reduced while the appreciation for other purposes in life would increase.

I am confident that these four years of leave would provide a higher degree of social security than today because the number of those who failed to make it in the system would decline. In the Economy for the Common Good, enterprises would not strive to downsize the number of employees in order to increase profit. In general, new employees would be more welcome in enterprises than they are today. Moreover the enterprises would join forces to help those willing to work to actually find a job; the legal incentives for doing so would be in place in any case. As the system dynamics would prioritize giving rather than taking, the systemic result would not be scarcity but rather plenitude. And in addition the large majority of the working population would be much more highly motivated to work because they would be allowed to help shape and participate in the success of their enterprise. Finally, the motivation to engage in the production process would increase as well because working hours and the work environment would be more humane in general. In light of such changed conditions, the need for unemployment benefits, emergency assistance and income support would be considerably reduced.

SOLIDARITY INCOME

Nevertheless, a sort of solidarity income for individuals who, despite searching hard, do not find any occupation, in the range of for example two thirds of the minimum wage, should be considered. The practice of the Economy for the Common Good would show if it is needed or not. In keeping with the democratic approach of the Economy for the Common Good, a guaranteed basic income or a Common Good currency ("Gradido")[26] could be an element of the economic order. Let the best alternative be found and implemented!

For people with special needs or restrictions who cannot engage in gainful employment at all or can do so only to a limited degree, there should also be a guaranteed basic income, sufficient to allow them to live their lives in dignity.

SECURE PENSIONS

Coupling pensions with financial markets was one of the greatest political mistakes of the neoliberal era. The hope of profiting from capital income – albeit to a relatively insignificant degree – which was held by broad sections of the population blurred one of the fundamental conflicts of interest in capitalist society, namely that which prevails between the minority which appropriates the lion's share of all capital income and the minority which generates and pays for it.

Privatizing pensions does not make them more secure, more socially equitable, or less expensive – in fact the opposite is true on all three counts. I have researched and discussed this issue elsewhere.[27] For this reason I would like to propose this alternative: in the Economy for the Common Good the discredited intergenerational contract would be rehabilitated and the time-proven contribution-based model would be strengthened. This would certainly be possible, despite the widespread belief to the contrary generated by propagandistic brainwashing – as the feasibility of contribution-based pensions depends on not less than ten regulatory measures: level of income, increase in productivity, labour force participation rate, unemployment, wage share in national income, rate of contribution, tax grants, state of health, pension entry age, and life expectancy. Demographic change, which poses insoluable problems for the profit-based model, could be cushioned completely by adjusting several such measures if the contribution-based model were used.[28] The population has been ageing rapidly for over a hundred years but this never caused a financial problem for pensions until the private insurance sector spread what is probably the greatest myth (the demographic time bomb), cashing in on it. In the Economy for the Common Good there would be no more profit-oriented banks and insurance companies; the financial system would become a public good. This is one important reason why (contribution-based) pensions would be secure. For all other aspects of social security, like childcare benefits or maternity pay, the welfare state would remain the same in the Economy for the Common Good.

To sum up, the "core" of the Economy for the Common Good model consists of redirecting economic activity towards a values-based, co-operative system, turning money into (a) a mere means and (b) a public good; streamlining the use of financial profits according to these new values; fostering cooperation instead of "counter-petition"; giving priority to ethical entrepreneurs, investors and consumers; and lowering the significance of gainful employment relative to other social dimensions of life, without lowering the level of social security. Some key elements of a complete economic order are still missing: the financial system and, especially, banks, as well as the case of property. The next two chapters will deal with these issues.

THREE
THE DEMOCRATIC BANK[1]

The Economy for the Common Good requires an entirely different financial system to the one in use today. The liberalization and globalization of financial markets have made banks appallingly inefficient – measured in terms of their benefit for society and the common good – and these developments have also diverted them to a perilous degree from their (supposed) core task, this task being to convert savings into loans and make these available to local enterprises, households and communities. Profit-oriented global-player banks fail to perform such core tasks to a satisfactory degree, if at all. They:

- cannot guarantee savings;
- loan money at expensive rates or not at all (creating "credit squeezes");
- increase account management fees and in some countries, such as the UK, close current accounts if customers refuse to buy stocks or bonds;
- thin out their network of branch offices and reduce basic services providing personal customer care.

Instead they do business which:

- undermines the stability of the financial system: leveraging, issuing derivatives, credit trade, currency speculation;

- create bank money, although they are only supposed to convert existing savings into loans, and thus contribute to the inflation of the money supply and consequent financial bubbles;
- redistribute resources from the masses to the moneyed via high-yield funds, exorbitant bonuses and dividends, abetment of tax evasion, assistance in building up large structures and concentration of power;
- encumber the state by allowing it to rescue them with taxpayers' money instead of making the owners (shareholders) accountable for financial losses.

Closer inspection reveals that "global financial markets" are a contradiction in themselves; on liberalized markets banks tend to strive for a globally competitive size. This is even the express goal of the EU's internal financial market and the world market for financial services in the framework of the World Trade Organization.[2] But this automatically makes them "too big to fail", which in turn means that several fundamental market rules cease to hold: (1) bankruptcy: system banks are condemned to live forever; (2) fair competition vanishes.

The "market" as such ceases to exist for other reasons as well:

- savings are guaranteed by the state;
- state-run central banks take responsibility for refinancing banks;
- system stability is also ensured by the state;
- shareholders are not liable when system-relevant banks go bankrupt, but rather the taxpayers are.

To make matters worse, the power of these "global players" has increased to such a degree that they can successfully protect themselves against fragmentation, regulation and taxation. They want neither a market nor a democracy. The detriment they do to the common good outweighs the benefits they bring. They are not only economically but also politically system-relevant ("too big to jail") and as such they are detrimental to democracy.

For this reason the Economy for the Common Good would be founded on an entirely different financial system. Money as credit would become a public good and the financial markets would be closed. This is what would happen to the individual gaming tables in the global financial casino:

- **Asset management.** There would be no more funds. People would deposit their financial assets at the Democratic Bank, a common-good-oriented cooperative bank or a savings bank which only did deposit and lending business. People would live on earned income, not on capital income. In return, their assets would be secure and stable. They would be guaranteed without restriction.

- **Stock markets.** Regional common good stock markets would replace central capitalistic ones. They would finance enterprises but not trade them. Dividends would be non-financial and oriented to values and goals of economic activity (rather than to means). Stock companies of the future would list regional (for example foodstuffs, energy) or global (for example software, high-tech) enterprises with citizen participation, a commitment to ethical conduct, a real purpose and the willingness and ability to generate use values.

- **Government bonds.** If they even still existed (I have made a proposal for an alternative form of financing public debts in another place),[3] they would no longer be traded but instead would be merely held with democratically fixed interest rates. The Democratic Central Bank would take charge of financing the public debt – up to a defined cap – on an interest-free basis.[4]

- **Investment banks.** Derivatives such as loan securitizations, credit default swaps (CDS), commodity and currency derivative debits would no longer exist.
- **Rating agencies.** If shares, bonds, credits and derivatives were no longer tradable or in existence, such ratings would be unnecessary. The agencies would be unemployed.
- **Futures exchanges and commodity markets.** Commodity prices would be fixed democratically by a commission of producers, consumers and representatives for future generations who would meet at eye level and negotiate humane prices for all sides.
- **Currency markets.** The "globo" or "terra" would be introduced as the world trade (or reserve) currency and the exchange rates of all national currencies would be "flexibly fixed" to it (following a proposal made by John Maynard Keynes).⁵ The Democratic Bank would exchange currencies at a uniform exchange rate.

This way the major "gaming tables" of the global financial casino, that is, the global financial market, would be closed. The core functions of the financial markets would be fulfilled by the Democratic Bank and regional common good stock markets as well as by further measures taken to achieve more equitable distribution of income and capital.

GOALS AND SERVICES

The Democratic Bank would be committed to the common good rather than to profit gain. Its values and goals would be identical to those of the Economy for the Common Good. In particular, regional economic channels and socially and ecologically sustainable investments would be promoted. The Democratic Bank would provide the following core services:

1. unlimited guarantees on savings;
2. a low-cost current account for each resident (that, with positive money reform, would be totally safe against losses);
3. inexpensive loans for enterprises and private households in cases of (a) economic solvency and (b) creation of ecological and social added value through investments;
4. a full-scale network of branches with respectful personal customer care in synergy with the Democratic Postal Office, the Democratic Railway Company, public internet docks;
5. inexpensive supplementary loans to the state and brokering of government bonds;
6. currency exchange.

These goals and services could be laid down in the constitution with the stipulation that they could only be changed by the owner itself – the democratic sovereign – by referendum. The government and parliament would have no access to the Democratic Bank. Directives and regulations (of the EU or the WTO) which stood in opposition to sovereign regulation of the bank would have to be abolished.

TRANSPARENCY AND SECURITY

All business conducted by the Democratic Bank would appear on the bank's balance sheet; establishment of branch offices or special-purpose entities in tax havens would be prohibited. The Democratic Bank would not be allowed to issue money (cf. the term "positive money" coined by Joseph Huber and James Robertson);[6] its role would be limited to handling money between savers and borrowers. The bank would be obligated to adhere to legal equity regulations but allowed to operate on the time-tested principle of good faith of the traditional banking system and to adopt anti-cyclical lending policies in times of crisis.

If the situation were to become more difficult for enterprises in such times, the Democratic Bank would be more generous. It would have sufficient capital to do so. It would fulfil a macroeconomic purpose – contrary to an approach seeking the maximization of self-interest.

FINANCING, REFINANCING, BANKRUPTCY

The bank would finance itself through lending fees to cover its costs (including credit losses, which on average would amount to less than 1 percent of the credit). The employees of the Democratic Bank would have a high degree of social security and comprehensive co-determination rights. They would make a decent living – as with all "democratic commons". The maximum income spread between the top and lowest-paid earners within the bank would be 1:10. Such a maximum degree of inequality was agreed upon for all public banks by the Parliament of the Swiss Canton Aargau in early 2013.

The bank would grant loans by drawing on deposits from private persons, enterprises and the state. Since these financial assets are growing steadily in relation to GDP, sufficient credit would be available (for refinancing measures).

Should the savings of a community, region or federal state prove insufficient for covering all socially and ecologically purposeful credit applications, other banks whose savings deposits exceeded the credit amount would distribute these to other banks. The Central Bank would accept liability for the risk of such distribution. It would act as the "ultimate lender". It is highly unlikely that any branch of the Democratic Bank would go bankrupt because:

1. the bank would not be profit-oriented, thus constituting a low-risk business;

2. its business activity would restrict itself to the "conservative" credit business; it would not trade securities and/or derivatives;

3. legal security regulations hold for granting loans;
4. the executive board would be personally liable if they did not abide by the laws;
5. a supervisory board elected on a direct democratic basis would monitor and control the activities of the executive board;
6. the executive board would also be accountable to the sovereign people and could be unelected at any time.

Nevertheless individual cases of bankruptcy could occur if a large number of loans were to be lost simultaneously. In such an event the Central Bank would prevent bankruptcy through recapitalization. The Democratic Bank would be "too essential to fail", just like schools, universities, railways and hospitals. Such institutions cannot go bankrupt today either.

INTEREST AND INFLATION

There would be no interest rates for loans or savings in the conventional sense. The borrowers would pay a loan fee rated in such a way as to allow the bank to cover its costs including investments and payments into a fund for social projects. Beyond this, credit costs would not generate profit for the bank or provide income for depositors.

The "real" Bank for the Common Good, which is currently being set up in Austria, will pay a moderate interest rate on savings initially. It encourages its customers to do without interest on savings from the very start, however, so as to make it possible to carry out socially and ecologically valuable projects whose credit costs would be reduced in this way. It actively informs people of the effects of the interest rate system.

In various publications I have elaborated three main reasons why I am in favour of eliminating interest altogether:

1. About 90 percent of the population lose out as a result of the
    interest system because they pay more for credit interest than
    they gain in savings interest. But most people do not realize this
    because the banks do not inform them of such costs. On World
    Savings Day all we hear about is the interest on savings deposits
    which we receive. The fact that we pay for this interest ourselves
    through our daily purchases because credit users add their credit
    costs onto the amount they demand for their goods is something
    banks conceal from us. It is as if they only showed us one side of
    the balance sheet. On World Savings Day the Democratic Bank
    would hand out a "personal interest calculator" which could be
    used to calculate whether you belonged to the small elite of net
    interest winners or to the large majority of net interest losers.
    Then a constitutional majority of interest opponents would soon
    be found.

2. Capital income of all kinds, not only interest on savings, triggers
    a compulsion to grow because credit users must pay back more
    money than they borrow. The carrying capacity of the earth
    has already been exceeded, however. The ecological footprint of
    humankind is already larger than the planet can handle long-
    term. Systemic drivers of growth should be removed from the
    economic order.

3. Mathematically speaking, it is not possible for the interest yield
    of the sum of savings deposits to match even the degree of
    inflation in the longer run. Every year in which the growth of
    monetary assets exceeds that of the real economic output – and
    this happens whenever (a) the savings rate or (b) the rate of
    return on capital exceeds the growth rate – a larger part of the
    annual economic output is needed to pay the same amount of
    interest on the monetary assets. Let me illustrate this point: if
    the monetary assets were currently one hundred times larger

than the real economic output, the entire GDP would be needed to pay interest on the monetary assets at a nominal rate of 1 percent. If there were an inflation rate of 1.5 percent, it would no longer be possible to preserve the value of the monetary assets. Mathematically speaking, interest claims can no longer be redeemed once a certain (multiple) ratio between financial assets and GDP (in "mature" national economies) has been reached.

Therefore the Democratic Bank would inform the public about the consequences that interest on savings in particular and returns on capital in general would have for the national economy and society at large, and they would prepare society for the end of "idle" capital income. Instead of using phrases such as "Let your money work for you" to erect a wall of fog between savers and their investments, the Democratic Bank would encourage savers to "Look and see what is happening with your money".

Since in the Economy for the Common Good there would be no more compulsion to grow, inflation might indeed vanish. This would also solve the problem of currency devaluation, and loans would be even cheaper if no interest had to be paid on the savings deposits to "compensate for inflation".

SOCIAL AND ECOLOGICAL CREDIT ASSESSMENT

When loans are granted, knowledge of the local situation and the entrepreneurial protagonists should play a role, not some anonymous rating. Credit applications would no longer be assessed exclusively in terms of economic profitability but rather in regard to their added social and ecological value. For this Common Good Creditworthiness Assessment, legal regulations would be applied, just like those for economic credit assessments. The principle of a Common Good

Creditworthiness Assessment would be similar to that used for the Common Good Balance Sheet which the Bank for the Common Good project is now developing on the basis of existing instruments. Planned investments with a particularly large social and ecological added value would be awarded loans free of charge or even with "negative interest", that is, they would not even have to pay back the full credit sum. In contrast, borrowers whose projects merely met the minimum legal requirements would pay correspondingly high charges for credit. Projects that created a reduced social or ecological value – for example stalls for thousands of animals or a nuclear power plant – would get no loan at all even if they were highly profitable business operations. The ethical guidelines would be elaborated by the economic conventions and decided by the sovereign people. In this way the financial market would finally also function as a steering instrument for socially and ecologically sustainable development. "Ethical investment" would become a legal standard.

ECO-SOCIAL VENTURE CAPITAL AND COMMON GOOD STOCK MARKETS

Projects whose profitability is uncertain hope to find financing options on stock markets and in other segments of the venture capital market but such markets lack any social and ecological awareness. A risk department of the Democratic Bank could adopt this function, devoting itself exclusively to innovations with an added social and ecological value. Each Democratic Bank could set aside a small percentage of its savings deposits for use as eco-social venture capital. A democratically elected ethics commission could decide which projects were particularly worthy of being funded and grant loans to them. Greater precautions could be taken for such projects.

A second – more market-oriented – possibility would be to establish regional Common Good stock markets which could be supported by all the banks in the region. The mechanism would be as follows: credit applications that were ethical but failed to pass a financial credit assessment would be passed along to such a stock market. People could participate in the project directly if the enterprise served a good purpose, generated use values and furnished proof of ethical conduct (via a Common Good Balance Sheet). Companies from the region that were certain of the project's success in terms of these criteria could go straight to the stock market. The advantage for the entrepreneurs would be that they would receive equity free of charge. The advantage for the financial investors would be use values and being able to have a say in a project with a social and ethical purpose. These would be the motives for making investments in the future.

SUBSIDIARITY, DEMOCRACY, REGULATION, TRANSPARENCY

The Democratic Bank would have a subsidiary structure. Most of the loans would be granted at the communal level. The Democratic Banks would make decisions autonomously. At the communal level the board would be elected on the basis of direct democracy, just like the supervisory board (the Democratic Bank Council) which would be in charge of overseeing it. The Democratic Bank Council would be made up of employee representatives, consumers, debtors, small regional businesses as well as gender equality officers and an ombudsperson for the future. All bodies would be filled with an equal number of women and men and reflect ethnic diversity goals.

The state or federal level would be responsible for large-scale investments and governmental loans but they would be proportionately co-financed at the local level. Excess savings deposits would be passed on to these higher levels as required. In case of excess wealth, financial assets could also simply be deposited in banks – if there were no real socially purposeful use for them.[7]

Representatives of local banks would elect the executive board and the supervisory board at the state level from their own ranks; these bodies would in turn elect the executive board and the supervisory board at the federal level. Head offices would only be responsible for liquidity equalization and for granting large-scale loans. They would not trade in securities, derivatives or any other assets. The state and federal levels would not be hierarchically placed over the communal level but rather have equal rights, constituting autonomous elements of the Federation of Democratic Banks. All elected representatives would be accountable to the sovereign people and could be de-elected by it at any time. All bodies of the Democratic Bank would meet in public.

Transparency coupled with co-determination would be a central feature of the Democratic Bank. Transparency generates trust. The balance sheet along with all credit transactions would be accessible to the public – with only a few well-defined exceptions.

Private accounts and money transfers would be subject to data protection, however. Only tax-relevant data would be automatically transferred to tax authorities (as is currently done with earned income in many countries). This regulation would have to apply for all banks so as to prevent the Democratic Bank from being at a competitive disadvantage.

RELATIONSHIP TO PRIVATE BANKS

So as not to subject the Democratic Bank to unfair competition, other banks would only exist in non-profit-oriented legal forms such as cooperatives and savings banks. Investment banks would cease to exist. During the transitional phase the following governmental guarantees and advantages would only be provided to common-good-oriented banks:

- deposit guarantees;
- refinancing through the central bank;

- business with the state;
- recapitalization in the event of insolvency.

Whereas profit-oriented banks would be left to their own devices on the free market, with all these governmental forms of support being withdrawn. During a second transitional phase the requirements could be tightened, with government support being granted to Democratic Banks, savings banks and cooperative banks alone, assuming they operated strictly in accordance with the following Common Good principles:

- no dividend payments;
- no interest on savings;
- Common Good assessments for all planned investments;
- limited eco-social venture capital;
- higher democratic standards.

To initiate the transitional phase, an EU-wide ethical banks' association could be set up whose members, as compensation for their Common Good orientation, would have a clearly reduced regulatory burden. After all, ethics should pay off.

THE CENTRAL BANK AND GLOBAL COOPERATION

The Central Bank would be organized in a new, transparent and democratic way. As part of the democratic bank system it would be the property of the sovereign people. The steering committee would be made up of representatives from all realms of society. The Central Bank would have a monopoly on money creation, putting limited amounts of the money it created at the disposal of the state – limited, that is, in such a way as to keep the relation between GDP and money supply more or less constant and prevent any acceleration of inflation. The Democratic Central Bank would finance the state via two channels:

- interest-free loans amounting to up to 50 percent of the GDP;
- unique gain from the conversion of private bank money into public central bank money in the dimension of the money supply M1 (in the UK: 78% of GDP in 2014);
- expansion of the money supply as a donation to the national budget (in line with GDP growth).

Only the first point, elaborated in detail in the "sovereign-money reform"[8], would downsize the UK's public debt from 89% of GDP (2014) to 11,2% of GDP.[9] The rest could easily be converted into interest-free loans from the Bank of England. This way the state would save the whole interest charge for the national debt which amounts to 48 billion pounds in 2014/15 and will continue to rise to up to 65 billion pounds by the end of the decade.[10] Together with the seignorage benefit after the positive money reform, this conversion benefit would balance the budget of the UK![11]

The division for global cooperation in the democratic bank system would grant inexpensive or no-cost loans in the framework of development assistance. The costs for this would come from the general tax coffers or through legally restricted money creation. The division for global cooperation would assume the default risk for venturesome exports that created added social and ecological value, promoted sustainable development and had passed an inspection verifying this. The means for financing such projects would also come from general tax money.

GLOBAL CURRENCY UNION AND GLOBO

The Central Bank would participate in a global currency cooperation following an idea initially developed by John Maynard Keynes.[12] The crucial elements of such currency cooperation would be:

- The creation of a common unit of account for international trade, that is, a global reserve or global trade currency (for example the globo or terra).
- This would be based on a large basket of currencies or commodities.
- National currencies would continue to exist. Exchange rates for the global reserve or global trade currency would be fixed by a global commission of the Central Banks and defended against any possible residual speculation.
- In the event of changes in real economic fundamental data (inflation, productivity, current account) the national currencies would be appreciated or depreciated with respect to the global trade currency so as to preserve economic parity (the "Greek tragedy" could have been prevented by depreciation, and the imbalance between the USA and China never would have developed).
- Whoever resisted appreciation/depreciation would be required to pay penalty interest for deviations from an equal balance of trade, with the amount increasing with the size and duration of the deviation.
- Cross-border payment transactions would be handled exclusively by public clearing offices operated by the Central Banks. This would allow effective prevention of tax evasion.

The Commission of Experts of the President of the UN General Assembly on Reforms of the International Monetary and Financial

System chaired by Joseph Stiglitz supports the proposal put forward by Keynes as an "idea whose time has come".[13]

REGIONAL MONEY

The globo would be a "complementary currency" at the international level. Complementary currencies could exist at the local level as well to promote regional business cycles and to enhance the resilience of regions in times of crisis. The Democratic Banks could issue such regional complementary currencies in their function as Regional Central Banks. The local democratic sovereigns would decide whether the regional currency in question should become legal tender with – regionally restricted – duty of acceptance.

CONCLUSION

Through political determination of exchange rates, commodity prices and interest rates (in the form of charges for credit) financial *markets* would cease to exist; the global financial casino would be closed, the formation of bubbles would be a thing of the past. The stock markets would be transformed into regional Common Good institutions through which equity from the region would flow, being channelled into the most useful enterprises. In this way, money would be forced back into its serving role. It would become a means for meaningful economic development and the common good. No one could become rich through possession of money alone; income would be made by working and for this reason such earned income would be enough to lead a good life.

WHAT ARE WE WAITING FOR?

At its activists' assembly in April 2010, Attac Austria adopted a project paper on the Democratic Bank.[14] It describes the idea of a comprehensive public bank. Since one cannot expect this idea to be implemented in the near future given the current form of democracy, Attac has called upon civil society to found a private prototype which could become a model for the foundation of similar bank projects. The Democratic Bank Project was initiated in June 2010, and since October 2010, the time of the actual launch, some two hundred persons have participated in it.

Renamed as the Bank for the Common Good Project (Projekt Bank für Gemeinwohl) the project has undergone a visionary process of its own, the result of which does not align on all counts with the ideal proposed here. This does not matter, however. What matters is that people who desire a different kind of bank could found it according to their own notions. Good progress has been made on preparations for founding the bank and if everything goes according to plan, the proposed Bank für Gemeinwohl will initiate operations in 2016.

FOUR
PROPERTY

The Economy for the Common Good would on the one hand be a completely ethical market economy and on the other a truly liberal one. The latter would mean three things: (1) all human beings and market participants should enjoy the same liberties, rights and opportunities; (2) the economic power of the one must be limited where identical or other liberties of fellow human beings are at risk of being encroached upon; (3) concerning property, which can be the foundation for liberty as well as for power and domination, diversity would be key. There should be a mixture of private property, public property, social property, communal property (commons) and use rights. No form of property should be given absolute precedence.

In the current economic order the absolute status of private property has come to pose the greatest threat to democracy. Through non-restriction of property rights some persons and enterprises have become so wealthy and powerful that they dominate the media and guide political processes to their own benefit. This contradicts the basic democratic principle of equal rights, opportunities and possibilities of participation for all. It also goes against the fundamental liberal principle that the freedom of the one ends where it begins to encroach upon that of the other – and thus also upon equality. Both principles imply that power in the state, in society and in business may not be distributed too inequitably lest such power be abused. In recent years numerous authors have addressed this issue, among them Robert Reich (*Supercapitalism*), Gerhard Schick (*Powereconomy*), Lisa Herzog (*Freedom Does Not Only Belong to the Rich*), Richard Wilkinson (*The Spirit Level: Why Equality is Better for Everyone*) and, most recently, Thomas Piketty (*Capital in the Twenty-First Century*). But even prominent proponents of capitalism such as the OECD secretary-general Ángel Gurría or World Economic Forum founder Klaus Schwab are also pointing out the dangers posed by the rise of economic inequality and are demanding restrictions.[1]

NEGATIVE FEEDBACK

The core idea behind the principle of the division of power is essentially that power in government must be divided (for example between the legislative, the executive and the judiciary) so that none of these authorities may become too powerful. Today we face the urgent necessity of transferring this principle to the economy because in this realm power is so concentrated that the excessive (property-based) freedom of the one endangers that of others. To achieve the necessary separation of powers I propose "negative feedback mechanisms". The term "negative feedback" is a concept from systems theory which means that a tendency that prevails within a system – for example warming – is cancelled out by a reverse tendency – in this case cooling. If this were not the case the system would overheat and explode. Negative feedback keeps complex living systems stable. "Positive feedback" means that tendencies reinforce each other. The melting of the Arctic ice sheet, for example, can lead to darkening of the land surface and thus to increased warming of the Earth, the result being that climate change will accelerate. Capitalism is a system with positive feedback because a progressive increase in wealth and size makes it easier and easier for individuals and enterprises to get richer and bigger. The first million euros is the most difficult one to obtain. Generating the second million is already a lot easier. Once a person has reached the 100 million mark he or she probably does not even really know any more how the last million was accomplished. Whoever has amassed one thousand millions has to spend a daily average of 220,000 euros in order to keep from getting even richer.[2] Negative feedback would mean that the first million would be the easiest to acquire and thus be obtainable for the majority, whereas getting even richer and bigger would be increasingly difficult until it became utterly impossible. The following forms of "negative feedback" could achieve this:

- limitation of income inequity;
- caps on the right to acquire private property;
- limitations on the size of company assets in the form of private property;
- limitations on the right to inherit.

LIMITATION OF INCOME INEQUITY

If I ask the highly diverse audiences at my lectures what the maximum difference is between how much two different people can get done in an hour, I get very consistent responses; they typically say one person might be able to achieve twice, five times or sometimes ten times as much as the other. If someone suggests it could be twenty times as much, there is usually a lot of headshaking. And when asked what the maximum difference between what two different people should be allowed to earn for the same duration of effort should be, the response is usually a factor of three, five, seven, ten, twelve or twenty. Some individuals suggest a hundredfold or thousandfold difference, while others advocate a factor of two or even one: the same pay for the same degree of exertion per time unit. Today the best-paid manager in the

USA, John Paulson, earns 350,000 times the statutory minimum wage, raking in an annual income of US$5 billion. In Germany, Porsche CEO Wendelin Wiedeking made 6,666 times the minimum monthly pay (hypothetically defined as 1,000 euros). Now most studies which address this topic come to the conclusion that such extreme differences:

- promote neither performance nor responsibility;
- do not make the rich happy but instead greedy;
- make the poor feel inferior (in every sense);
- foster discomfort, stress, illnesses and mortality;
- lead to a rise in mistrust, aggression and crime.[3]

Beyond a certain threshold, inequity does not benefit society any more at all; instead it begins to be a detriment. As pleasant as doubling the outside temperature from 13 to 26 degrees Celsius might be, the warmth becomes quite unpleasant if it rises to 39 degrees, and every additional degree aggravates the discomfort even more. Warmth is not a goal in itself, but merely a pleasant condition if the optimum (of well-being, quality of life) has been reached. In the case of economic inequity there is no "natural" optimum, but human beings have an intuitive sense of justice and it is only logical that their sense of justice is offended if someone gets 350,000 or even "only" 6,000 times the pay that someone else gets for doing the same amount of work. According to a survey conducted by the *Financial Times* and the Harris polling firm, 78 percent of respondents in the USA were of the opinion that inequity had increased too much. In the UK, 79 percent thought so; in China, 80 percent were of this opinion, and in Germany 87 percent held this view.[4] These responses are presumably distributed among voters of all large parties. Another survey revealed that 81 percent of Germany's conservative Christian Democrats (the CDU) think managers' salaries are too high.[5]

The proposal of the Economy for the Common Good is to have a democratically organized economic convention work out several possible limits for income inequity, for example a seven-, ten-, twelve-, twenty-, thirty-, hundred- and thousand-fold multiple, letting the population vote on the issue using the systemic consensus principle.[6] If the most ambitious wanted to earn more, this would be possible; the only thing is that the minimum wage would have to increase as well. The rich and the poor would be fatefully intertwined. An important addition is that the minimum wage would have to guarantee conditions of life fit for human beings. It could be attached to a "good-life basket" with the standard net income being somewhere in the vicinity of 1,250 euros in Central Europe, $1,500 in the USA, or £1,000 in the UK.

Since no capital income would exist in the Economy for the Common Good, the problem of adding together earned and capital income would be eliminated. Rent income would be added on to personal income and the total would be limited, for example, to ten or twenty times the minimum wage. Theoretically enterprises could pay their employees more, but the maximum tax rate would reach 100 percent from a certain democratically fixed multiple of the minimum wage upwards. Hiding income or assets from the tax authorities would no longer be possible since the (common-good-oriented) banks would automatically report all income to them. International capital transactions would be overseen by the Democratic Central Bank. This way the only possibility remaining would be to have millions paid out in cash and stuffed inside a pillow. But then the money would be missing on the balance sheet, and the pillow would soon become so big it would fill up an entire room.

RESTRICTION OF PRIVATE ASSETS

Have you ever tried to spend a billion dollars? You would need a large staff of helpers to master this enormous task. You would have to devote an increasingly large part of your day to "managing" your assets, becoming, in a sense, an employee of your own fortune. Those who possess too much become obsessed. Happiness research has shown that material wealth only increases life satisfaction up to a relatively low level, beyond which life satisfaction is enhanced by other values. But this is not the main problem (because a free society should never take away anyone's right to self-inflicted unhappiness). The main issue is that persons who accumulate billions and billions amass enormous power and thus have immense leverage when it comes to influencing society (and thus impairing the happiness and freedom of others). What billions are capable of doing can be illustrated by looking at Silvio Berlusconi (the media oligopoly), George W. Bush (with his oil empire) or Frank Stronach (who bought a political party in Austria). If individuals are granted unlimited right of ownership the freedom of the majority will suffer – or even be eliminated altogether – because in a society with extreme inequity mistrust, fear, violence, crime and corruption increase. The epidemiologists Kate Pickett and Richard Wilkinson have collected a plethora of studies on this topic. One of the conclusions they draw is:

> if the United States was to reduce its income inequality to something like the average of the four most equal of the rich countries (Japan, Norway, Sweden and Finland), the proportion of the population feeling they could trust others might rise by 75 percent – presumably with matching improvements in the quality of community life; rates of mental illness and obesity might similarly each be cut by almost two-thirds, teenage birth rates could be more than halved, prison populations might be reduced by 75 percent, and people could live longer while working the equivalent of two months less per year.[7]

For this reason an upper limit for private property would have to be discussed in the Economy for the Common Good, for example ten million euros (once again, the economic convention would have to decide). Ten million euros is still so much that anyone who possessed that amount would be able to afford almost any luxury and yet that sum is not enough to buy a government or to shape society according to one's own will. In other words, property rights would be quite liberal!

DEMOCRATIZATION OF CORPORATIONS

A deeply rooted reflex reaction many people have when someone criticizes the power of private property is to reproach that person for allegedly wanting to get rid of it. But that is just as illogical as it would be to suggest that someone who advocates longer lunch breaks wanted to eliminate work altogether or that mobility researchers who espoused speed limits had an aversion to motion.

Entrepreneurs such as carpenters, craftsmen, innkeepers, software programmers, architects and florists all have private property but they do not endanger the freedom of others because they do not possess the political power necessary to do so. For this reason such small enterprises should be allowed to keep all of their private property in the future as well (even if they are rewarded for conduct which promotes the common good). Small and medium-sized enterprises constitute the large majority of all enterprises. In Austria, 99.6 percent of companies have fewer than 500 employees. Multinational corporations are quite another matter, however. Today global groups exist that are more powerful than many governments. Their decisions have the potential to affect hundreds of thousands of people and they exert a disproportionate influence on the media, political parties, science and justice. The fact that a few private individuals determine the course taken by such giants while all those affected – inside corporations and beyond them – are given no say is profoundly undemocratic. This situation is irreconcilable with the highest good in Western culture, namely democracy. For this reason, large corporations should be democratized to ever higher degrees in proportion to their growth in size, and the degree of co-determination granted to society should be increased accordingly. Take this possible scenario, for example:

- in enterprises with over 250 employees the workforce and society get 25 percent of the voting power;
- in enterprises with over 500 employees they receive 50 percent of the voting power;
- in enterprises with over 1,000 employees they have two-thirds of the voting power;
- in enterprises with over 5,000 employees the voting power is distributed evenly among the owners, the employees, the customers, the gender equality officers and the environmental ombudspersons.

In some countries, such as Germany, employee co-determination already exists in large corporations; the largest challenge is still to achieve co-determination of society, although this already exists as well: the State of Lower Saxony in Germany holds a 20 percent blocking minority in Volkswagen, and this is certainly not to the detriment of the company. But state property managed by governments is a source of unease for many people, and rightly so. Depending on the government in office, such enterprises could be guided in various different directions and in the worst case misused.

Thus it would be better if society had a body independent of government which helped steer the enterprises. One could conceivably have a regional economic parliament which would act as a representative of the sovereign people and be on the supervisory board of all large companies in the region. This parliament would be elected by means of a direct democratic procedure. The "democratic supervisory boards" would have to be highly qualified in terms of business management, ethics and as Common Good customers. They would have to draw up regular reports, elucidating how they exercised their right to vote for the benefit of all. This would create an economic–political public which would concern itself not with the development of stock prices but rather with the satisfaction of needs and the purposeful allocation of investments.

If the public and the employees were to take more responsibility the larger a company became, it would only be fair for them to help bear the brunt of any financial losses. Freedom and responsibility should be coupled. During the bank and economic crisis of 2008 the situation was such that private owners made the decisions and the general public bore the losses. This is just as unfair as the reverse would be. For this reason the public sector should adopt financial responsibility as well, to the degree that it has a say in decision-making processes. If it had no desire to take such responsibility for any given company, it could reduce the company's size again, thus "fully privatizing" it. Private owners would be at liberty to do the same. If they wanted to make all the decisions themselves they would have to keep the company correspondingly small. In Austria only one enterprise in a thousand has more than 500 employees. If the proposed threshold values were applied, 999 out of 1,000 enterprises would have majority private control and majority private property.

EMPLOYEE PARTICIPATION

For as many people as possible, the long-term goal of the Economy for the Common Good would be for them to become co-owners of the enterprise they work in and to take mutual responsibility in guiding its operation and bearing the risk of loss. Democracy means not merely having a say in matters but also bearing mutual responsibility and risk. For this reason even small companies should be rewarded for doing this – but not be obligated to do so – if they allow those employees who desire to do so to participate in the company and bear the corresponding responsibility and risk. An argument often raised is that not everyone would want to do this; but everyone would not have to. No one could claim, however, that there are no employees who would like to be part-owners of a company and also take financial responsibility! Those who did could be offered the opportunity to do so by the transfer of 1 or a few percent per year of the company's property to an employee fund, for example, which the employees, as full-fledged owners, would have a say in. If enterprises did this, they would get bonus points on their Common Good Balance Sheet.

RETAINING PROFITS IN COMPANIES

According to current law, owners of an enterprise can appropriate the entire profit earned by all its employees. Those who support this legal situation justify it by citing the right to property and by arguing that the owner brought capital into the company (initially) and took the concomitant risk of capital loss. His or her legal responsibility and liability are also cited. Indeed, the owner of a company often does work more for it than the employees do, but sometimes also the owner does less.

As a company increases in size, nevertheless, the contribution which non-founders make to the profit it earns increases as well; no one would contest this fact. For this reason the profit should not go exclusively to the founder indefinitely, particularly since in the long run this person is only responsible for a (shrinking) part of its success; the degree to which the owner should be entitled to the profit should indeed decrease to the degree that the efforts of others are responsible for the success of the company. The following scenario would be conceivable: for companies

- with more than ten employees the proportion of profit the founder could appropriate or pay out in dividends would decrease by 1 percent each year;
- with more than twenty employees the proportion would decrease by 2 percent;
- with more than thirty employees the proportion would decrease by 3 percent;
- with more than fifty employees the proportion would decrease by 4 percent;
- with more than one hundred employees it would decrease by 5 percent.

In other words the founder of a company with over one hundred employees would no longer have access to any of the profits after twenty years. An important distinction must be made here: we are talking about the balance sheet profit and not the entrepreneur's income! As before, founders of companies could be paid a salary which exceeded the statutory minimum wage by a multiple of ten or twenty, for example. The idea put forth here would have no effect on most small enterprises. The objective would be to protect large companies from excessive profits being skimmed off, especially by inheritors who had not built up the enterprise but now owned it and appropriated part of its profit whether they worked or not. Today many family-owned businesses already refrain from distributing profits (paying out dividends) and they do it out of principle. They voluntarily practise the highest level of conduct proposed here because they already embrace the notions that (a) profits should stay in the company and (b) everyone who works should receive remuneration for doing so, including the owners of enterprises.

On the other hand many people found companies with the motive of providing for their old age. For this reason an exception to the rule "no capital income" could conceivably be made. Founders of enterprises could be allowed to derive a (limited) pension from the earnings of the company founded and built up by them over many years. For example one could decide that anyone who built up a company for twenty-five years could receive a "company founder pension" for an equal period of time. This would be in addition to the statutory pension, which would already suffice to live out one's life in dignity along with the savings that had accrued in the course of building up the company. The amount of the supplementary company founder's pension would be adjusted to the amount of money the founder had taken out of the company while building up the enterprise. This is the core idea: whoever scrimped and saved to establish a company should receive a higher company founder's pension than someone who remunerated himself generously for his own efforts from the very start, was able to put quite a bit of money aside for this reason and was thus already well provided for in old age.

RESTRICTION OF THE RIGHT TO INHERIT, GENERATIONS FUND AND "DEMOCRATIC DOWRY"

Inheritance tax also serves the purpose of preventing the accumulation of huge assets in the hands of a few.
Constitution of the Free State of Bavaria, Germany, paragraph 123

An unlimited right to inherit annuls the only "natural" negative feedback mechanism of capitalism, namely that by which accrued and concentrated assets get deconcentrated and redistributed. Thus it perhaps poses the single largest impediment on our way to a democratic, liberal society pledged to providing equal opportunities for all.

The effect of an unlimited right to inherit is that some of us enter working life with a starting capital of several billion euros while others begin with nothing (and, in some circumstances, with emotional trauma and a lack of self-esteem). In the USA and the UK, the fact that many students are obliged to take out loans to pay for their studies means that many young people begin work having already amassed a huge debt. According to the Institute for Fiscal Studies, the average British student debt will be £44,015 at the end of his or her studies. An incredible 73 percent will be unable to pay back this debt in their lifetime.[8] In Germany, at the beginning of the millennium, only 15 percent of the adult population received an inheritance.[9] Thus 85 percent did not benefit from the right to inherit. Since high concentrations of property constitute a power factor, the economic injustice is combined with a political injustice. Just compare the possibilities for political participation that are open to the offspring of welfare recipients with those offered to the heirs of ABF, Stemcor, Porsche or BMW owners and CEOs. Who will be more successful in life? Studies on the elite show that the managers of tomorrow are not necessarily the most talented and intelligent people, but rather the sons and daughters of today's managers. Some 80 percent of the managers working in the hundred largest corporations in Germany come from the richest 3 percent of the population. In 2003 only one CEO of the 30 DAX-listed companies had a working-class background. For this reason Michael Hartmann, a researcher who studies the elite, writes: "Managers are already born as such."[10]

Would it not be fairer and promote performance more if everyone were to start out under the same conditions? Regarding the right to inherit, sober consideration elicits two extreme positions:

1. **The feudal position.** Birth alone decides who inherits what and how much. Talent, performance and equal opportunity do not

count. This is the basis for the current – unrestricted – right to inherit in Germany and Austria.

2. **The liberal position.** All start out under the same conditions, and performance alone decides who will acquire greater assets and who will not. This position presupposes either complete abolition of the right to inherit or equal distribution of inherited property to all.

The Economy for the Common Good would avoid such extremes. It would neither embrace the feudal principle to an unrestricted degree nor would it abolish the right to inherit completely. The solution would lie somewhere in the middle; the right to inherit would be applicable up to a democratically fixed maximum sum, with assets exceeding that sum going to a public Generations Fund and being distributed to all members of the next generation in equal parts in the form of a "democratic dowry".[11] The limit for financial and property assets could lie at 500,000 or 750,000 euros per person, for example (the values to be discussed and decided upon by the economic convention).

In Germany, inherited assets amount to an annual sum of 130 to 200 billion euros[12] – which are approximately one fiftieth of the total national assets (11.3 trillion euros).[13] If this amount were to be evenly distributed to all those starting out in working life, that would amount to as much as 200,000 euros per person – not a bad starting capital!

Of course, the sum would be reduced if inheritances amounting to up to 500,000 or 750,000 euros were not distributed and thus not "democraticized" either. The lower the threshold, the larger the amount to be distributed via the Generations Fund. This fund could transfer the democratic dowry to all citizens at the age of entering professional life. Those who did not inherit anything by this time would get the full "democratic dowry" of, for example, 100,000 euros. Accordingly, those who inherited 15,000 euros would receive the democratic dowry minus the inherited amount, as a form of "negative inheritance tax" (similar to a wage bonus paid to reach the minimum wage level). For every year in which the national assets increased, the average democratic dowry would increase too. In contrast, if an unlimited right to inherit were preserved, the starting conditions and thus the power relations would become increasingly unequal. There would soon be some people with trillion-dollar inheritances and many have-nots.

REAL ESTATE

The fact that a good half of personal wealth exists in the form of real estate assets is the only weighty argument for preserving the right to inherit private assets up to a certain limit. If it were not for this, one could abolish the right to inherit altogether and provide everyone with an equal "democratic dowry" when they started out so as to achieve at least initially equal financial opportunities. In the case of real estate property this would not be advisable, however, since inhabited flats and houses would have to be relinquished, which is not exactly humane. But an exemption of 500,000 euros would already almost solve the problem. According to the Austrian National Bank, (a) only 50 percent of all households own a real estate property and (b) only 5 percent of the population owns a house with a value of over 450,000 euros.[14] In the UK, the exemption threshold for inheritance tax lies at £325,000, which is a little less than 500,000 euros. For Austria, a 500,000 euros threshold would mean that only 5 percent of the population would be affected by the limitation on the right to inherit. In this case a property owner would have to decide whether to share the inherited house (should it have a value exceeding 500,000 euros) with another inheritor (who would also be allowed to inherit a property worth 500,000 euros) – hence a house with a value of 850,000 euros could be passed on to two children, for example – or an owner who wanted to own such a huge house singly would have to pay the amount which exceeded a value of 500,000 euros into the generations funds for the benefit of society in general. Today this actually happens quite often: a piece of real estate is left to several children in equal parts but is taken over by one of these children, who then pays out his or her siblings' shares.

Of course, the sovereign people would be free to define a higher exemption amount, for instance 750,000 or one million euros, to minimize this issue.

INHERITANCE OF ENTERPRISES

Now comes the greatest challenge: inheritance of enterprises. Today all enterprises, even global corporations of unlimited size, can be bequeathed to children completely tax-free in most European countries. Education, talent, performance and social responsibility play no role here. This is extreme.

And this is why, already in 1924, Winston Churchill called inheritance tax "a certain corrective against the development of a race of idle rich".[15] In subsequent decades, inheritance taxes reached historical ceilings near to 80 percent in the UK and the USA, whereas by today the top rates have dropped back to only 40 percent.[16] This fact has evoked responses from such prominent critics as the US billionaire Warren Buffett, who compared poorly restricted inheritance with "choosing the 2020 Olympic team by picking the eldest sons of the gold-medal winners in the 2000 Olympics".[17] Inheritance law currently works in exactly this way. The consequence of an almost unlimited right to inherit is that most enterprises built up by entrepreneurs today will be run tomorrow by persons whose only "qualification" is that they are the son or daughter of the previous owner. The latter need not even be the founder of the enterprise; he or she might have merely inherited or bought it. This phenomenon has little to do with an achievement-oriented society in which everyone should be able to develop assets through his or her own efforts and his or her own contribution, and it has just as little to do with a democratic society in which everyone should have the same opportunities to participate and find the same social protection in business. In the Economy for the Common Good the goal would be to ensure that enterprises' assets are held by as many people as possible in order that as many as possible can help carry responsibility. For this reason democratic entrepreneurial structures would be promoted, and one can presume that the proportion of cooperatives and similar legal forms of business would rise. In such cases the issue of inheritance would not be raised at all since cooperative shares are usually very small.

Privately held companies would not pose a problem either because shares would be viewed as financial assets. If such shares exceeded the limit for inheritance of private assets they would flow into the generations fund. Another special case would be privately held companies founded by a person's own parents.

Thus the only really tricky thing would be family enterprises. As a compromise between a liberal position (equal opportunities for all) and (quasi-feudal) family-oriented tradition, inheritance law could be designed here in such a way that family members would be allowed to inherit shares in the company amounting to a maximum of five, ten or twenty million euros (start values). Any shares exceeding this amount could:

1. become the collective property of the employees who bore responsibility for the enterprise and helped develop it (unlike some owners); for this solution Common Good points would be awarded;
2. go to selected non-family-members who were willing to bear responsibility for the enterprise. In this case the share would once

again be limited to 500,000 or 750,000 euros and would count as a "democratic dowry";

3. flow into the generations fund, being distributed in the form of "democratic dowries" to individuals who wanted to work in the company and would own a small part of it, bearing of course a part of the risk.

4. For agricultural assets a special regulation could be found, which will be discussed later (see "Ownership of nature", page 103).

A family business that was run by five family members could thus be inherited by the offspring up to a value of 50 million euros "tax-free". Despite such a compromise this proposal continues to elicit strong emotional reactions. The counter-argument often raised is that parents would have no incentive to build up an enterprise if they could not pass it on to their children in its entirety. Were this to be the case, it would also be proof that human beings do not act out of purely egoistic intentions, as is often imputed, but rather exert themselves for the benefit of others – their children. According to this logic, childless individuals would have no incentive to do anything at all. This is diametrically opposed to the ideology of the market economy which has prevailed for the past two hundred years, the claim being that everyone strives for his own benefit and advantage and that this is what we hope to derive maximum motivation and system efficiency from.

We all know there are entrepreneurs who have no children or whose children do not want to take over the business. It is not uncommon for the question of succession to divide the minds of entire (sometimes quite extended) families. In such cases the enterprise could be transferred to those who work in it and wish to take responsibility for it together with debts owed by the company as well. Should there be children, they would be entitled to the full "democratic dowry" if they decided not to accept the inheritance. Speculative buy-ups and immediate resale of estates (to private persons) could be prohibited by stipulating that an individual would only be allowed to inherit a share in the company if he or she had actually worked in the business for at least three years. Enterprises are not toys; they should be controlled by those who are willing to adopt personal responsibility and create added value through their own exertions.

What is the objective of these proposals? Fairer distribution of company property, democratization of enterprises and thus ultimately the replacement of capitalistic conditions by more democratic and more liberal structures. For in total, the freedom of the individual would not be limited by these proposals but rather increased. The "loss of freedom" of the heir who is not allowed to inherit Mama's and/ or Papa's large corporation alone and run it irrespective of his or her qualifications to do so would be countered by the gain in freedom on the part of countless people who currently begin their working life today with no inheritance or means at all (even if their parents helped build up an enterprise through decades of work).

Today such people might even find work in a company inherited by people who have done nothing to contribute to its development but who now own it and proceed to appropriate the added value generated by the work of others who have inherited nothing and must work for them as a result. In other words, we have a case of structural slavery. Today the only alternative non-inheritors have to selling their own labour power is to set up a successful company themselves. Not everyone is in a position to do so, however – for diverse reasons and often through no fault of their own. And in capitalism the top dogs do not make it easy for newcomers. Thus many are forced to work for others and to hand over to them the added value produced by their own work. This makes capitalism a systemically unfree and exploitative structure. The objection one could raise, namely that everyone has the possibility of becoming an entrepreneur and that for this reason those who do not take advantage of this option should be willing to work for others, is out of touch with reality because some people simply do not fulfil the prerequisites for founding a business. Equal opportunities do not exist because human beings differ in terms of their health, their talents, their education and their assets. These many forms of inequality are no fault of their own.

Arguing that "everyone could if they only wanted to" is not even logical because if everyone were to take an entrepreneurial risk upon themselves, which is always claimed to be a matter of free volition, there would be no "dependent workers" any more. Then no one could hire even one employee or apprentice; division of labour in the market economy would not work any more. Thus the contribution that "dependent workers" make to the economic product is just as indispensable as is that of the employers and for this reason it should be esteemed in equal measure and remunerated similarly or – ideally – organized in a better way. This would entail co-participation and co-ownership for all who want it instead of having a minority decide everything and being allowed to appropriate the added value generated by others on the basis of the wholesale justification – apt or erroneous – that they contribute more, take more risks, and carry more responsibility. In systemic terms it would be more logical and fairer if:

1. decisions were made by all employees and investors mutually;
2. earnings were distributed among all employees/value-adding protagonists;
3. as many as possible had a share in the property, and
4. as a result helped bear the entrepreneurial risk and responsibility.

An automatic retort made in reaction to those proposing more democracy in enterprises is: "But many employees do not even want to take any responsibility!" and: "Not everyone is able to run a business!"

But they would not have to. They would only have equal rights in regard to determining who should run the enterprise. Running a typical small business with five employees on a direct democratic basis would be no problem. In cases of large enterprises with, say, three hundred employees there would certainly be some who "only" wanted to do their work. And why should they not be allowed to do this? But they should have a say in who should make the decisions in the enterprise. Then it would be run by people and not by capital.

Coming back to the issue of family businesses, if they were passed on not exclusively to owners' sons and daughters but rather to a group of democratic owners, that would hardly mean that the sons and daughters would have no chance to (help) run the business. They would simply possess no automatic, dynastic entitlement – like succession to a throne; instead the children would have to prove themselves deserving of such a responsible position by applying for it and convincing the workforce that they were the candidates most suitable for the tasks of management. This means that in the Economy for the Common Good sons and daughters could take over and run quite large family enterprises founded by their parents or grandparents – but only if they were the people best suited to do this. Remember what Warren Buffett said. If others were better, the right to inherit would no longer automatically equate entitlement with ownership and management. Realizing this and acting accordingly would constitute taking a long overdue step out of the feudal ages – a step not yet taken because of intensive ideological indoctrination.

The proposed measures would create two kinds of negative feedback in regard to one of the central problems of our time: unequal distribution of capital and the excessive economic and political power of global corporations and individuals which accompanies it. This twofold negative feedback would be achieved through in-company democratization and progressive communalization of enterprises as they grew in size. The result would be a more democratic and freer economy. More people would have a say, the opinions and competencies of more people would be sought, and the value of more human beings would be appreciated to a degree not previously reached – not only in the form of a commendatory pat on the back but through material property and co-determination rights.

Almost everything said here has already been thought and written by many others, for instance the famous John Stuart Mill, whose *Principles of Political Economy* was the leading textbook in economics in the second half of the nineteenth century:

> The inequalities of property which arise from unequal industry, frugality, perseverance, talents, and to a certain extent even opportunities, are inseparable from the principle of private property, and if we accept the principle, we must bear with these consequences of it: but I see nothing objectionable in fixing a limit to what any one may acquire by the mere favour of others, without any exercise of his faculties, and in requiring that if he desires any further accession of fortune, he shall work for it.[18]

ENDOWMENTS

Some people might object that the proposed limitations on rights of inheritance could be easily circumvented, for example by mothers and fathers giving multi-millions to their offspring during their own lifetime. Such efforts to get around laws could be easily prevented, however, by introducing an endowment exemption equal in sum to the inheritance exemption. Parents could opt to give their children 500,000 or 750,000 euros, for example. But such endowments would be deducted from the inheritance, as is partly foreseen in the British

Inheritance Tax Act. Some might argue that parents could still hire their own children and pay them exorbitant salaries for their work. This type of circumvention seems improbable to me, however, because it would come up against various hindrances and limits, for example:

1. earnings being allowed to be no more than 10 or 20 times the statutory minimum wage;
2. a 10 million euro limit on private property;
3. parents would have to push through extremely high salaries against the possible resistance of others with a say, and this would become harder and more unlikely to succeed the farther along democratization had progressed;
4. shares in enterprises would not necessarily be paid in the form of a "cash" salary. Parts of the company would have to be sold, which would increase the probability that it would be democratized.

Of course in introducing a new social and economic order we should give some thought to how efforts to get around this order should be penalized. But nothing provides such strong proof of our capacity to do this as do property rights. Whoever wants to "get around" today's protection of private property must reckon with severe prosecution, punishment and imprisonment. Consequently the Economy for the Common Good would not have *more* property regulations and laws but rather *different* ones: minimum participation on the part of all would be protected as systematically as unlimited private property is for only a few today.

"DEMOCRATIC COMMONS"

In addition to a majority of small private enterprises and a minority of corporations with mixed ownership there should be at least a third category of property – namely private and public common property. I will talk about classical private commons later and start with public property. But not in the customary form. In Europe after World War Two, roads, railways, power supply mains, drinking water and gas utilities, schools, universities, hospitals, post offices and telephone lines were established and operated by the state. These were referred to as "public services". Since the 1980s this public sector has been liberalized and privatized to ever-increasing degrees. This process has perhaps reached its nadir now; bad experiences and protests have begun to turn things around.[19] My proposal is not to return to the kind of state-run utility companies we had in the past but rather to have essential branches of industry be controlled directly by the population. I have introduced the concept "modern commons" into discussions on this idea.[20]

Traditionally speaking, "commons" are a common good that belongs to everyone. During the Middle Ages these were typically an expanse of forest or meadow which could be used by all inhabitants of the village. Using this historic fact as a source of inspiration, "modern" or "democratic" commons could be railways and the postal services, universities, utility companies and kindergartens or even banks. Sovereign proprietors would take charge of these businesses, running them themselves. International examples of success in this area show how this could work. In Sacramento, the capital of the state of California, a power supply company called SMUD provides 1.5 million people with electricity. The executive board of this energy supplier is elected on the basis of direct democracy. For this reason the enterprise must orient itself to the priorities of the population, which it does excellently. In terms of environmental protection and high-quality service, SMUD is highly preferred by the population, constantly ranking at the top nationwide and performing way above statutory minimum standards in California. The owners get to decide on the most important issues themselves. So far this in-company form of direct democracy has been applied once:

in 1989 SMUD asked its citizen owners whether the company's only nuclear power plant, Rancho Seco Nuclear Power Generating Station, should continue to operate – with lower fees, but the risk of a nuclear accident – or if instead a new path should be taken in the direction of alternative energies, what would increase user fees. The majority of the service's consumers decided in favour of decommissioning the plant and making massive efforts to promote green energy sources. Looking at California's environmental record today, we can clearly see the success of this "sovereign" decision.

The Swiss population landed a similar success for the environment via direct democracy. In the 1980s the government wanted to make ruinous cuts in the operations of the state-run railway system and to privatize it in a fashion similar to Germany or the UK. But in Switzerland the sovereign people vetoed this plan. Through a referendum demanded by the population, the billions earmarked for road construction were reallocated for expansion of the railway system. The result is that Switzerland now has the best and most popular railways in the world.

A third example: in the Brazilian metropolis of Porto Alegre the communal budget is drawn up with participation of the population ("participatory budget") and the municipal drinking water supply is organized via a "public popular partnership", or PPP. The municipal administration and the population work together in this alternative PPP. The result is just about as sensational as the one achieved in California: 99 percent of the population is connected to the drinking water network and the rate of sewage connection has now reached 70 percent. Because the wealthy people who water their golf courses and fill their swimming pools have to pay highly progressive rates, the poor are provided with inexpensive drinking water and the public-owned enterprise gets by without any subsidies from the municipal budget, which is to say, without a single cent of taxpayers' money.

With regard to the organization of the "democratic commons", I envision a directly elected executive board made up of representatives of public authorities (the government), employees and consumers as well as gender equality officers and environmental ombudspeople. "Classic state-owned enterprises" that are controlled by the government or the mayor should not exist in the Economy for the Common Good. A public services convention could define those areas of business which should belong to the public Common Good sector along with the rules for organizing it.

"Classical" commons are privately organized, and range from pastures and fishing grounds to seed farms and software. The Commons Strategy Group around David Bollier and Silke Helfrich have done extensive work on this.[21] The first female "Nobel laureate" in economics, Elinor Ostrom, has also written on the rules that must be respected if commons are to work well and not end in "tragedy", as predicted by classic economics.[22]

OWNERSHIP OF NATURE

Humankind did not create nature – neither the flora nor the fauna. Human beings can use nature but if they are not careful, they will destroy the foundation of their own existence and themselves. We are guests on this Earth who are merely tolerated on a certain condition, namely that we possess ecological empathy. Respect for nature could be expressed by agreeing that no individual should own any part of nature, particularly not any land.[23] But those who require land for concrete aims or for purposes of cultivation should be allowed to use a limited amount of it at no charge. Especially among farmers who have become accustomed to "owning" a bit of land this mindset might make them feel unappreciated in their fruit-bearing labour. But they would still "possess" some land; it is just that its ownership would be returned to nature. Nothing would change for agriculturalists in terms of their tasks and practices. In fact everything would become cheaper because land tax would be eliminated. This would be an expression of the community's appreciation of their valuable labour. In return the amount of land allocated to each person as productive land would be limited. In concrete terms the situation could be this:

1. Municipalities would regulate allocation of productive land.
2. Every individual would be entitled to a living area up to a certain limit, for example a maximum of 10,000 square metres. Use of such an area could be acquired for a certain fixed square-metre price. These areas could be exchanged for other areas of a similar size but only for the purpose of living on them.
3. Agricultural businesses would be allotted a certain amount of land free of charge on condition that they cultivated it with care. Here the Common Good Balance Sheet could influence the size of the land furnished for productive use, for example. This would constitute an additional regulatory mechanism of the Common Good Balance Sheet.
4. Enterprises from all sectors – similar to private persons – could acquire land needed to set up offices and production sites for a utilization fee. In return, land tax could be eliminated.

The effect of these measures would be that:

1. appreciation for nature would be promoted. Ecuador was the first country in the world to attribute an intrinsic value to nature, the Pacha Mama, in its constitution of 2008.[24] Something which has an "intrinsic value" cannot be the "property" of others;
2. the extremely inequitable distribution of real estate property would be reduced;

3. intestacy rules regarding farmsteads would be simpler because there would be no more owned land but only allocation linked to cultivation, and landholdings would not have to be divided up among heirs. Tax on landed property would also be eliminated;
4. real estate speculation and land grabbing, two logical consequences of illiberal capitalism, would become a thing of the past.

LIBERTY AND EQUALITY

In pseudoliberal capitalism the right to property is viewed as one of the supreme liberties which should, as such, be invested with absolute status. Yet equality in the sense of all human beings having the same rights, opportunities and liberties – has a higher value than freedom because too much freedom for the one can endanger the freedom of others. If I drive too fast ("freedom of movement"), insult others ("freedom of opinion"), injure someone ("freedom to rampage"), or buy a million hectares of land, I limit the freedom of others – to the point of endangering their lives. Thus equality is an absolute principle and freedom a relative one. Restriction of freedom is a principle but restriction of equality is not. In respect to property this means that all human beings should be equally entitled to a limited amount of property (enough to lead a good life) but no one should have unlimited right to property. Once the most extreme form of inequitable distribution were reached, that is, if one person were to own the entire world and there was nothing left for all the others, even the last sceptic would probably agree with this train of thought. Freedom is important, but what is even more important is that everyone has an equal right to it.

FIVE
MOTIVATION AND MEANING

MOTIVATION

One of the most frequent worries people have the first time they hear about the Economy for the Common Good is that motivation would slacken in business if enterprises did not pursue boundless financial gain, people did not primarily strive for their own benefit, and competition were "eliminated": after all, where else should performance incentives, innovation and prosperity come from?

These fears stem from the capitalistic, that is, social Darwinist image of humankind according to which human beings are primarily motivated by egoism and competition: if there is no competition to fear people only work half as hard or lie around doing nothing; they do not really know what to do with their lives if they are unable to compare themselves to and compete with others, if they are not driven by the fear of losing their status or by a craving for prestige and superiority. Intrinsic motivation, childlike curiosity, inspiration and spontaneous creativity hardly have any place in this image. Before I address such apprehensions and show why they are scientifically unsound – even though each of us knows people who are primarily motivated by egotism – I want to start by taking quite a pragmatic approach.

1. The most frequent and simplest motivation for participating in an enterprise or founding one in an Economy for the Common Good is that people need monetary income all the same. The necessity to earn money is not eliminated altogether even though it is mitigated, especially since people get four free years in addition to the "democratic dowry" and a reduction of working hours. The solidarity income (see Chapter 2) is enough to survive with dignity but not to lead a "good life". Those who want to lead a good life must do something for it but the framework in which they go about achieving this will be completely different and much more favourable with regard to finding and accepting gainful employment than it is today because in the Economy for the Common Good (a) people will have more of a say in things because the roles of "entrepreneurs" and "employees" will become increasingly indistinct; (b) people will find more meaning in gainful employment; (c) people will be less stressed and overtaxed; and (d) enterprises will not compete with (or against) each other and be forced to make higher profits than the others, which will mean that they will not cut jobs to stay competitive.
   In cases of structural unemployment the Economy for the Common Good will be adapted in such a way as to reward companies more if they hire additional people.

2. Incomes from private enterprises will still be allowed to amount to a certain multiple of the statutory minimum wage; the exact amount will be decided by the sovereign people. Thus for people who are very interested in having money there will still be an incentive to accept work or to open up a new business. Since the minimum wage will be calculated in such a way as to allow persons to live in dignity – for example with a net income of 1,250 euros per month in Central Europe , $1,500 in the USA or £1,000 in the UK – anyone who desires to have a lot of money

has the possibility to earn ten or twenty times the amount that is necessary to lead a good life. Since hereditary rights are limited and possession of assets is no longer rewarded – only work is – it can be ensured that income does in fact accrue through actual performance. To obtain higher incomes it will really be necessary to do more. Owning assets will no longer suffice.

3. Happiness research has shown that beyond a certain point high incomes do not make people happier and thus cannot constitute any purposeful motivation. According to international studies the threshold lies at an annual income of US$20,000, which is hardly any more than the assumed statutory minimum wage of 1,250 euros per month.[1] The highest threshold known to me is an annual income of US$290,000[2] – which is about twenty times the proposed minimum wage. Increases in income that exceed this figure do not generate any verifiable increase in happiness (or in performance: the 45 best-paid Toyota managers each earned an average of 320,000 euros in 2009.[3] Would anyone claim that Toyota vehicles would be better if the managers earned 3.2 million euros? Or 3.2 billion for that matter?)

4. Not only happiness researchers but also sociopsychological and neurobiological scientists have come to the conclusion that human beings are more strongly motivated by factors other than money: among other things through strivings for autonomy, identity and competence, the desire to make a contribution, community and relationships.

- **Autonomy.** Human beings strive for freedom in the sense that they want to be able to perceive and articulate their feelings, needs and thoughts freely. No one wants to be restricted in their fundamental human existence. "Money" is not essential to anyone because it does not constitute any feeling, basic need or creative thought.

- **Identity.** All human beings are unique, and one possible meaning of life consists of discovering one's uniqueness and allowing it to unfold. What counts is not being *better* than others but rather being *different*. What counts is not being better at the same thing but rather being unique in terms of what one has to offer.
- **Competence.** Recognizing, nurturing and developing dormant abilities are a basic need. We should be facilitated to do so. This works in cooperative structures just as well as in competitive ones.
- **Making a contribution.** Every human being has something to contribute to the whole, and every human being wants to contribute something. Community and plenitude arise from the contributions of all.
- **Community.** Human beings are community-oriented. They would rather die than be isolated from other human beings even if they had food.[4] Our brains are programmed for social networks. Communities fulfil further basic needs such as a feeling of security, safety, esteem, approval and a listening ear.
- **Relationships.** "Meaningful relationships are the unconscious goal behind all human endeavour," Joachim Bauer writes.[5] This is the conclusion that current neurobiological research has arrived at.

When giving talks I assess such insights time and again by asking my audience to reflect for a moment and name the situation in which they have felt the most happiness to date. What people name are moments of connectedness and experiences of successful relationships on four levels:

1. a meaningful relationship with oneself;
2. meaningful relationships with other human beings;

3. a meaningful relationship with nature;
4. a meaningful relationship with the larger scheme of things.

The keywords most often cited – apart from intense experiences in nature such as walks on the beach, sunsets, mountain peaks and garden work – are "birth", "friends", "partnership" and "love", namely fulfilling interpersonal relationships. In business such experiences could also constitute goals to be defined, valued and financially remunerated. We would not be very wise if we failed to apply the scientifically verified "expertise" or collective experience of happiness and meaningful community in business as well. In the Economy for the Common Good, letting meaningful interpersonal and ecological relationships thrive would invest performance and economic success with a new meaning. In the end we would not only aim to reach a goal that has a social purpose but we would also, as evidence shows, be more highly motivated than we are by the current competitive structures and the pursuit of personal benefit at the cost of others. Democratization of enterprises will increase not only the motivation of all those involved but also their prosperity: "If a company is transformed into a community through a larger degree of co-determination then productivity will increase as well." This is the assessment made by epidemiologist and inequality researcher Richard Wilkinson on the basis of numerous studies.[6] And he confirms the experience of Ricardo Semler with Semco in Brazil.[7]

The path may still be a long one. Today, owners of capital are still held in high esteem because they are viewed as persons who are willing to take a personal risk, create countless jobs and generate economic prosperity. What would things look like in an Economy for the Common Good? To start with, more and more people would have the possibility to found a company because they could start out with a substantial amount of start-up capital. They could immediately participate in companies or found new ones themselves. If several persons were to pool their "democratic dowry" they would soon have a million euros to found a business. Since the founders would not even need a bank loan, their entrepreneurial risk would decrease significantly. The following proposed measures would also play a role:

- progressive employee share ownership;
- progressive immunization of profit against dividend payouts;
- obligatory employee participation in large enterprises.

Just distribution of capital and votes leads to a more even distribution across the population of the willingness to take risks. Then the community is less dependent on shimmering personalities who are stylized as top performers even though some of their assets were merely inherited rather than earned, or were acquired through positive feedback effects at the cost of others. In almost all cases they also rely on the invisible relationship work of women whose essential, life-preserving and happiness-giving accomplishments are hardly recognized, valued or rewarded. Slowly but surely relieving entrepreneurs – primarily men – of their "sole responsibility" for a company would mean that the patriarchal fetters of society, which continue to be active today, would dissolve as well.

MEANING

One of the greatest strengths of the Economy for the Common Good would be that earning money would no longer constitute the goal, the side effects of which would be (assuming things went well) satisfaction of needs, prosperity and meaningful activity. It would be the other way around: satisfaction of needs, common good and meaningful activity would be the goal, and the founding and managing of companies would constitute means of fulfilling that goal. If participation in the production process and engagement in gainful occupation become easier in systemic terms (for the founders of companies as well as for persons employed by others), if the possibility of amassing material wealth is limited and if the climate of society as a whole promotes meaningful relationships then there is justified hope that more people will select their workplace in accordance with their potential for investing it with meaning and (be able to) shape it accordingly. And meaning is a powerful source of motivation, if not the most powerful one. It provides intrinsic motivation and has a stronger effect than does extrinsic motivation, which causes people to act through external incentives, rewards and punishments. If I decide to do something of my own free volition because I deem it to be purposeful then I usually do it gladly. I devote myself to it with all my energy and undivided attention. If I am intrinsically motivated to perform a task it does not occur to me to peer over to the left or right to see what "the competition" is doing. This would merely distract me, disturb my concentration and thus weaken my performance. (Unless of course I am someone who is spurred on to perform well out of fear or whose self-esteem relies on outdoing others.) Those who are extrinsically motivated are heteronomously reliant on the relative status of their competitors. Their motivation abates the moment they are superior to their competitors for, after all, it is not the activity itself which motivates them. And if someone loses out often or chronically, motivation will vanish as well. People withdraw from competition humiliated and end up in a state of unemployment, homelessness, depression and dire poverty. In the UK, 13.3 million individuals live in poverty, including one out of three young adults – 6 percent more than a decade ago in Britain.[8] In 19 out of 28 EU member states, youth unemployment rates have climbed to over twenty percent.[9] Market capitalism, if measured in terms of the expectation that it should provide all human beings with meaningful, humane work conditions, is in fact a system that is as inhumane as it is inefficient. Why then is the belief in the benefit of competition so deeply rooted and so seldom questioned?

What comes now is, from my perspective, the most unpleasant part of this analysis, the part which will allow us to understand why competition is so firmly enthroned in our value system. Many – possible the majority of us – are not intrinsically motivated (or at best to a very weak degree) because they do not know themselves well enough and do not discover any aspect of themselves that might spur them on to top performance without competition. They are empty inside and can only find meaning outside themselves. And if the outside world constantly clamours for money, a career, success and power, viewing these as the "values" that count, then they internalize many of these values even if these values have never made any human being happy. But since so many buy into this belief and the media constantly portray and honour such people, a large proportion of the population emulates them – people who have no real sense of their own selves. Thus the root of the problem lies in inwardly impoverished people who are incapable of investing their own lives with meaning; they lack the self-confidence needed to recognize themselves as being ultimately responsible for their own lives and their own decisions.

The crucial question is: Where does this inner emptiness come from? Why is it that so many people are incapable of investing their own lives with meaning and finding happiness? In my view the key lies in education. Most of us were not impartially *recognized* and unconditionally loved, which would have allowed us to find our own self, accept ourselves with love and develop the same deep appreciation for others; instead, many – at least the older generation – were raised to be obedient and perform well. If parents have a certain image, a concrete notion of how we should be, they will lose sight of who we really are. Children are not able to recognize themselves in otherness because they are not "mirrored" by their parents or, what is worse, are punished if they attempt to do so. In order to avoid losing the love of their parents, most children "decide" in favour of obedience, and the first "order" given by very many parents is that their children perform (and thus abnegate themselves). Thus children learn early on to suppress their own feelings, needs and thoughts – feeling, thinking and wanting what they *should* feel, think and want instead. Of course, this does not happen in extreme ways in the sense that children either just become motivated intrinsically and develop their personal meaning of life in full autonomy – or suppress their inner self and only adopt extrinsic values whilst clinging to the illusion that these values will lead them to happiness. But the societal tendency leads in this direction. And it is enough that culture hands down "extrinsic" values such as competition, profit seeking and careerism from generation to generation and that the majority of human beings now believe that this is their nature merely because the majority of those in their generation, who were raised to believe this way, behave accordingly.

Children who have not learned to perceive their own feelings, needs and thoughts but rather to be rewarded by "love" for obedience and performance will attempt to get love through performance for the entire course of their lives. They will not question what they are doing – or if they do, only half-heartedly – and will soon accept money for their accomplishments until they do practically nothing any more which is not financially remunerated. In this way money becomes the highest good for the inwardly impoverished. This explains why a remarkable number of rich people are inwardly impoverished to such a large extent.

A further consequence of all this is that those who do not have a sense of themselves lack a sense of others – and of the environment. Empathy requires a fine sense of self-perception. This is a crucial reason why successful men and women often have fewer scruples when it comes to pushing for economic "success" at the cost of social and ecological detriment. Inner emptiness desensitizes people and hardens them. The values inherent in the capitalistic system shape them into ruthless executors of the system objective – increasing profit – no matter the cost. (Bare figures are their only source of orientation. They must reduce themselves to what is calculable.) Socio-medical studies show that among top-tier economic decision makers – as compared to the average population – one finds a significantly higher proportion of socio-pathological personalities who are incapable of empathy and compassion, who are narcissistic and prone to addiction.[10] Such selection is a fatal effect of our current economic system, and more and more of those affected by this are beginning to realize and admit it. As the former head of the German Postal Service and tax evader Klaus Zumwinkel confessed, "In my twenty years as a chief executive I learned that markets are essentially soulless".[11] One of Austria's few female top executives, Brigitte Ederer, reports on the effects of her job: "You become harsher towards yourself and towards others."[12] Is this not a catastrophe?

To reverse the effects of such social conditioning, measures taken to reverse market incentives – promoting recognition, assessment and remuneration of cooperative, solidarity-based, empathic, responsible and generous behaviours – are not enough. We need to start by fulfilling the prerequisite for implementing these measures, which is that parents love their children unconditionally and accept and esteem them as they are. From a parent's perspective this certainly does not mean letting them get away with everything, allowing them to grow up without guidance or agreeing with all their opinions but rather it means (a) perceiving their feelings, needs and thoughts, (b) taking them seriously and (c) encouraging them to do so themselves. It is only then that we can ask what feelings, needs and opinions the parents have; in fact they are often quite different. But with the help of respectful and nonviolent communication it is possible to learn that different, in part contradictory needs and opinions exist which do not necessarily pose any insurmountable hindrance to communal life and meaningful relationships. On the contrary: since we are all unique and thus in principle different, relationships in which partners do not have differing needs and opinions are inconceivable. Thus we should always assume that our colleagues, partners, friends – and children – have different needs, feelings and opinions to our own and we should aspire to take these seriously and value them – rather than attempting to confrontationally assert our own opinions, needs and interests vis-à-vis others. We have now returned to the beginning of the book: to the aspect of mutual treatment under the guiding light of human dignity instead of the pursuit of one's own benefit. This interpersonal dimension is so fundamental that it should play a key role in our educational system.

CHILDREARING AND EDUCATION

One of the most important prerequisites and conditions for a flourishing Economy for the Common Good involves conveying new values, sensitizing people to their own human existence, rehearsing social and communicative competence, and setting an example when it comes to respect for nature. For this reason I propose seven basic subjects for all levels of school which I deem to be more important than most of the subjects currently being taught. They are: understanding feelings; understanding values; nonviolent communication; understanding democracy; understanding and experiencing nature; crafts; and sensitizing the body.

1. Understanding feelings

Here children would gain the experience of perceiving feelings, taking them seriously, not being ashamed of them, talking about them, and regulating them consciously. Nonviolent communication has shown that myriads of conflicts in relationships remain unresolved because human beings do not succeed in talking about their feelings and needs

– particularly if they have never learned how to do so. Instead they reproach those who do not fulfil their needs and thus trigger a sense of injury for all kinds of things which divert attention from their own needs and feelings, the actual matter at hand, hurting others in the process. An endless spiral of injury is the result, with the problem persisting and no prospect for a resolution of the conflict in sight.[13]

2. Understanding values

Here various attitudes towards values are taught and discussed in the sense of developing the critical faculty. This should also include making children aware of subconsciously held values. For example, children would learn that they are capable of competing against each other and what the effects of this are, but also that they are capable of cooperation and can see what the effects of this are too. In an overview they learn the fundamental ethical principles of various philosophical ideas and religions.

3. Nonviolent communication

Here children start by learning how to listen, heed others, take them seriously and discuss matters objectively without resorting to personal insult or value judgements. This might seem banal but we are aeons away from an appreciative and nonviolent culture of public discourse. Even opinion makers and prominent citizens in many realms adopt the wrong tone. For example, in the past Attac and I have been referred to by the media and public figures as "stuck in adolescence", "martial", "communist", "nauseatingly populist", "swaggering hero of anticapitalists" and also as "a spiritual mentor of terrorism". Apparently some opinion leaders are unable to tolerate different opinions. Yet a democratic and nonviolent culture of discourse is characterized by the very fact that we treat those who think differently with respect – by arguing exclusively on a substantive level.

In the class on understanding communication, children would also learn about differences in the ways men and women communicate so as to become aware of role patterns and thus become able to discard them. In the same way, intercultural communication skills could be taught. And, generally, that misunderstandings are the norm and generating understanding always takes a certain amount of effort.[14]

4. Understanding democracy

Democracy is viewed as the highest value in the West, and yet the way this value can be lived and sustained – through intervention, having a say and advancing co-determination in all areas of public life – is hardly a matter that is taught at school. Democracy is presented as a reliable historical fact, not as a fragile, vulnerable accomplishment which can be lost at any time. In fact, it can be argued that it has already been lost because the majority of people, having no means of participation, have turned away from the public sphere in disgust and frustration, and because other enticements – consumption, entertainment and drugs – are thrust upon them by an economic order which suffocates the spirit and is antagonistic towards the public and democracy.

Understanding democracy could include the following elements:

- how to incorporate many interests into one rule;
- how decisions are made that are as acceptable as possible for everyone;
- that appreciative encounters with others who have different needs are the prerequisite for satisfactory decision-making processes that are supported by a broad majority;
- that alert commitment on the part of all is required so that particularized interests cannot be asserted;
- that democratic responsibility cannot be delegated but rather only the power to implement decisions.

And most of all: that democracy has just begun. We have only savoured about one tenth of what is possible through democracy; the experience of "real democracy" – the motto of the Occupy movement – has yet to be created. More on that in the next chapter.

5. Understanding and experiencing nature

An economy that relies on persistent increases in profit, income, assets and material goods is sick in the sense that it has lost all sense of proportion; it is "absolute" and detached from all other values and their natural foundation, the planetary ecosystems. An inability to connect and the difficulty that many people have in relating to themselves, to other human beings, to their natural environment and to the larger scheme of things is the core of this illness. Healing can consist of re-embracing these relationships, nurturing them and bringing them into equilibrium, which is a reliable path to happiness. Countless human beings in all cultures report that having an intense, appreciative relationship to the environment, to living creatures, rivers, cliffs, clouds and deserts have a healing effect. Spending several hours in intense communion with nature will most likely mean finishing the day with a sense of elation. In this subject children will not only learn how to identify plants, animals, bodies of water and stones; they will also experience the healing effect that nature has on their peace of mind. Wind and rain, clouds and water, stars, flowers, the mountains, tranquillity – whoever has a deep connection to nature is likely to find little of appeal in shopping centres, the stock market, or even the possession of a car. In any case, experiencing a year of reduced material consumption can mean an increase in the intensity and quality of life – even though, from the perspective of classic market economists, this means a betrayal of the economy, destruction of production sites and recession.

6. Crafts

The "couch potatoes" generation spends an increasing amount of time in virtual space sitting at computers, talking on mobiles, watching television or using any number of other electronic devices and media. This virtual world separates human beings from the materiality of nature and the tasks devoted to manually processing it. One essential element of a holistic life lies in encounters with materials and substances, tools and shapes, colours and smells. We do not all have to become master craftspeople but we should all experience what it feels like to produce something manually and to give it to someone who can put it to good use. Rudolf Steiner, the founder of anthroposophy, advocated developing a comprehensive programme for enabling pupils to come into contact with the "practice" of life, and for this reason Steiner schools include internships in forestry, various trades and social institutions in their curriculum. It is important to provide sufficient time for these activities so as to connect the self with the task at hand and unfold the entire creative potential that young people have. Fashioning useful things oneself creates meaning, and making gifts makes people happy. And if some of these young people become master craftspeople or artisans, this is very beneficial for society.

7. Sensitizing the body

Che Guevara reportedly said: "Solidarity is the tenderness of the people." But how should all states treat each other with tenderness if we do not succeed in being tender to ourselves? Many of us eat badly, get too little exercise, show little physical affection, rarely massage ourselves or others even though this is one of the fastest ways to reach happiness for all the people I have met so far. If we compared the time we spend shopping, watching television and earning money with the time spent giving or getting a massage, the sad subordination of physical touch and tenderness would be revealed. The human body is an endlessly sensitive organism and we all possess the disposition that allows us to sense things so finely that each step and each contact with an object can lead to a deep sensual experience or massage of the inner self. With sensitivity training, the quality of life would increase to such a degree that there would hardly be any time left for nonsensual experience. The weaker the sensual element, the weaker physical self-perception is, the more these privations must be compensated for by money, power or other drugs.

For this reason children should be helped to develop a fine, attentive and appreciative relationship to their own body, their creativity and authenticity early on. This can begin with games, dance and group acrobatics and later, after puberty, be expanded to include elements of bodywork, massage, energy work and yoga.

SIX
ADVANCING DEMOCRACY

Democracy is the worst form of government,
except for all those other forms that have
been tried from time to time.
Winston Churchill

¡Democracia real ya!
Indignados

Genuine democracy is not a hollow phrase.
Albert Einstein[1]

Formally speaking we live in a democracy, but compared to the period before accelerated globalization and financialization, fewer and fewer people feel that they really have a say in any aspect of social life. There is an increasing tendency for governments to make decisions that contradict the needs and interests of the population at large. These involve such issues as:

- deregulation of financial markets, allowing for speculation against systemic stability and the common good;

- privatization of public services such as drinking water and energy suppliers, railways, postal services and banks;
- the unleashing of global site competition through "free trade agreements";
- liberalization of capital transfers to tax havens;
- tolerance of income inequality up to a factor of 350,000;
- implementation of gene technology in agriculture, legalization of patents on life forms;
- the Euratom Treaty;
- the commitment to rearmament in the EU Lisbon Treaty;
- repression of demonstrators at the Copenhagen Climate Conference;
- torture in Guantánamo;
- the attack on Iraq which violated international law;
- and since 2008 the bank rescue policies enacted for the benefit of large, system-relevant corporations without fragmenting them.

If procedures of direct democracy had been employed, in most countries there would likely have been no majority to back any of these decisions. And yet they were formally taken by democratically legitimized governments and parliaments. There are several reasons for the growing distance between the citizens and their representatives, which political scientists call "the crisis of representation".

1. A voter who can only elect a party platform every four or five years has almost no control over anything because election promises are just as inflated as they are non-binding. If governments do not fulfil the promises they make, we as voters are almost completely powerless. If we want to "punish" a government that has failed to fulfil any particularly important promise, we must wait for the next election. But even then, how are we going to sanction them?

Do we have to change parties to do this? Does any party even exist whose platform is more agreeable to us in total? What if no party is standing for election whose platform addresses the issues most important to us? And would the "punished" party even understand what it is being punished for as we have no avenues for taking it to task for any individual decisions it makes, but can only punish it for its performance during the legislative period as a whole?

2. The economic elite are merging with the political elite to ever-increasing degrees. Top managers often move into government and political office holders become lobbyists for large corporations through an ever-faster "revolving door".[2] One emblematic example out of many is the former EU Trade Commissioner Leon Brittan who became Chairman of the LOTIS Committee of International Financial Services London (IFSL), a lobby group representing the UK financial industry.[3] Another example is Sharon Bowles. As the chairperson of the European Parliament's Economic and Monetary Affairs Committee, she led important negotiations over EU rules governing the London Stock Exchange. In August 2015, Bowles joined the London Stock Exchange Group's board of directors as a non-executive director.[4] A very recent example is Jonathan Hill who was nominated by the UK prime minister David Cameron to become EU Commissioner purely for Financial Services and Financial Stability. Hill refused to hand out a complete list of his past interests as a lobbyist to the Members of the European Parliament.[5]

Thanks to the revolving-door phenomenon, the roles of regulators and the regulated become blurred. In the aftermath of 2008, the most powerful bankers drafted bank rescue bills and parliaments sign them. The problem with such social intimacy between politics and business is that it becomes more critical the richer and more powerful the economic elite become. This shows that the economic elite *themselves* constitute the problem – and this confirms the demand for limiting inequity. The material elite stand in contradiction to a democratic society in which all human beings should have equal rights, equal opportunities and equal possibilities for co-determination.

3. Such elites also have a disproportionate influence on the leading media: through personal contacts with senior journalists who cultivate such contacts so as to secure valuable sources of information, through values which they share with the media elite (since powerful people who are keen on keeping their power are highly cooperative), through advertising which the media are economically dependent upon and which they adjust their editorial line to, through direct control of property, and again, thanks to revolving doors. For instance, before its split in 2013, the supervisory board of Rupert Murdoch's News Corporation contained two former heads of government, José María Aznar from Spain and Alvarez Uribe from Colombia. Besides entanglement, media corporations become too concentrated and powerful: in the USA in 2011, only six corporations controlled 90 percent of the US media.[6]

4. Mainstream academia sometimes even subscribes to the opinions of those in power. To be sure, "free" universities provide space for alternative approaches, but the "mainstream" is confluent with the agenda of the powerful because (a) many intellectuals come from "good families" and promote the interests of their own "class"; (b) due to ongoing liberalization, universities are increasingly dependent on external funds from industry; and (c) private interest groups generate a lack of public funds but also take advantage of this lack by positioning their ideological propagators inside colleges and universities by installing guest

professorships. The University of Illinois's College of Agricultural, Consumer and Environmental Sciences (ACES) in Champaign-Urbana has accepted a $250,000 grant from genetically modified seed/agrichemical giant Monsanto to create an endowed chair for the so-called Agricultural Communications Program it runs with the College of Communications.[7] On the other hand, scientists whose insights endanger corporate interests are denied research funding, and may find their jobs and careers threatened.[8]

5. Think tanks work for those who fund them. These are usually influential economic circles whose needs have little in common with those of the population at large. In the USA, the American Legislative Exchange Council (ALEC) sounds smart and scientific, but in fact is a privately funded council of politicians and members of the business elite who actually write legislation and then have their members push for it in Congress. Meanwhile, in Germany, the nicely named New Social Market Economy Initiative is not so much a circle of intellectuals committed to the Enlightenment or ethics in business as it is a campaign instigated by powerful industrial employers' associations striving to dismantle the solidarity-based social welfare state.[9]

6. Political parties are financed by corporations, and in the USA the members of Congress are directly financed by lobbyists – with predictable results. Here are two examples. Members of Congress who voted for the regulation of financial derivatives received a total of only US$940,000, whereas those who voted against them received US$27 million. Those who supported regulation of the US Federal Reserve received US$40,000, whereas those who opposed it received US$10 million. The bill failed miserably.[10]

As a result of these conditions and developments, democracy is in serious crisis. If we allow the economic inequities, lobbyism and media concentration to persist and reduce "democracy" to the act of ticking a box for a political party every four or five years, it will inevitably erode to the point of dissolution. If a living democracy is to be created, the entwinement of politics and business must be dissolved and limitations must be put on inequity. What is equally needed, though, is an extension of democratic participation, plus rights of regulation never seen before in history. As many people as possible must be able to engage in discussions, participate in decision-making processes and help shape society at as many levels as possible, and they must be able to do this during the periods between parliamentary elections and in all democratic areas of social and economic life as well.

WE ARE THE SOVEREIGN!

The basic precondition for achieving a renaissance of democracy is the creation of an awareness of what the sovereign actually is or should be. The word "sovereign" comes from the Latin word *superanus*, which means "standing above all". Whereas during the age of absolutism the king was the Sovereign who stood above all, the Enlightenment and the bourgeois revolutions brought about the notion that the general population should actually have this role. Yet such theoretical entitlement hardly manifests itself in any modern-day democracy. The only sovereign rights that the citizens possess are to elect political parties and to have the final say in fundamental changes to the constitution. This is not enough to constitute genuine sovereignty. Genuine sovereignty would also entail the sovereign being able to:

1. elect a certain government;
2. de-elect a government;
3. correct its parliament in regard to any proposed legislation;
4. put bills to the vote itself;

5. change the constitution on its own initiative;
6. elect a convention directly;
7. control and regulate important essential utilities itself;
8. stake out the framework for negotiation of international treaties and vote on the results of such negotiations.

There is such a weak sense of what the sovereign should entail that most of us do not even realize that we, the public, lack the basic tools required to act as the democratic sovereign in our countries. We do not learn this at school. During lectures I often ask which instrument should be placed in the hands of a "sovereign" first. This question usually elicits awkward, widespread silence. Some hesitatingly say "elections"; others timidly ask: "passing a law?"

If the sovereign really "stands over all" and the only purpose of democracy is to implement its will – the common will of the largest possible majority – then the sovereign should be able to propose and pass laws by its own efforts at any time! But at present this is impossible in the individual member states of the EU, as well as in the EU as a whole, because our representatives have a monopoly on initiating laws. In the EU member states it lies with each nation's government and parliament and EU-wide it lies with the Commission, the Council and the Parliament. Supplementing indirect ("representative") democracy with direct democracy would constitute a logical implementation of the principle of separating power between the people and their representatives. A clearer separation of powers would make for a tangible increase in democracy and greater trust in this form of government.

EXPANSION OF THE SEPARATION OF POWERS

Fundamental principles rarely remain uncontested. The democratic principle of the separation of power is a fortunate exception. The division of state authority into the legislative, the executive and the judicial branches and reciprocal control thereof is taken as self-evident. We ponder too little on what the basic idea behind such separation of power really is, however. The objective is to prevent power from being too concentrated and thus subject to misuse. Hence, no institution should be so disproportionately powerful in relation to others as to endanger freedom – in this case collective freedom, which is to say, democracy. Since so much is at stake, the principle of separation of power merits the most intensive reflection and systematic advancement possible.

We have already begun to elucidate the first step required for implementing such advancement: more efficient division of power between the sovereign people and its representation. But why does a sovereign people elect representatives in the first place? Since a nation state is inhabited by so many people, it is not feasible to let everyone participate in the agreements it makes. Grassroots democracy has its limits, and these limits are defined by the number of people who can actively participate in the democratic process. Thus division of labour is the principle behind the election of governments and parliaments. The task is not to create a new organ which is placed over the sovereign people for its own sake; governments and parliaments are merely its representatives, whose exclusive purpose consists in implementing/ fulfilling the majority will of the sovereign people. There is no guarantee that any given government actually does this, however, and the temptation to misuse power which has been temporarily leased increases in proportion to the limitations put on the rights of the sovereign people and the unfettered clout which some interest groups continue to have vis-à-vis government. As Jean-Jacques Rousseau wrote in 1762: "Nothing is more dangerous than the influence of private interests on public affairs."[11] It would be ruinous if the hands of the sovereign contractor were to be bound until the next award of contract (election), it being left with no more than the feeble hope that government might fulfil its will. But this is an increasingly common scenario. Governments and parliaments are transformed into "temporary dictatorships" because they submit to the most pressing lobby groups, are infiltrated by them or even welcome them into their ranks. The overlooked sovereign people can protest and demonstrate but what good does this do if it has no rights? Does it not make more sense for the democratic sovereign – as the supreme actor – to be able to correct his agent at any time if the latter does not do what the former wants it to do? Rousseau felt that the sovereign should be able to "limit, amend and nullify the power which it bestowed on the government whenever it choses".[12]

A THREE-STEP DIRECT DEMOCRACY

In concrete terms this means, for one thing, that the sovereign population would have the right to reject any bills that it deemed unacceptable through a majority vote. And, second, that it would have the right to draft bills and pass laws which were not in keeping with the government's "agenda". Both rights could be asserted using the same procedure, namely a three-step direct democracy. This is an idea which a growing number of organizations are now demanding.[13]

- **First step:** every citizen or group of citizens could collect declarations of support for a desired bill.
- **Second step:** if this draft bill found a sufficient number of supporters, for example 0.5 percent of the population eligible to vote, a petition for a nationwide referendum would be initiated.
- **Third step:** if this petition – the collection of signatures at polling sites all over the country – made it over a further, larger hurdle such as 3 percent, an obligatory referendum would be held, the results of which would become legally binding law.

The "third step" is currently applied not only at the national level in Switzerland, but also in California in the USA. Here the citizens are the actual sovereign. In Germany, Austria, Italy and most other countries including the USA at the federal level, the parliament has the last word. And it has the capacity to go against the will of the people and build nuclear power plants, allow capital to flee to tax havens, legalize patents on life forms, rescue system-relevant banks with taxpayers' money, and participate in wars of aggression which violate international law.

Direct democracy is gaining ground all over the globe, however. From 1951 to 1960 a total of 52 national referendums were held worldwide; from 1991 to 2000 the number increased to 200, and in the first decade of the third millennium the number rose to about a thousand.[14] In Germany this instrument has been introduced in all the states in the 1990s and also generalized on the communal level. And in South Tyrol, Italy, an initial form of direct democracy is winning one stage victory after another. The first form of direct democracy was introduced in 2005 but it did not fulfil the expectations of the initiators in the population. For this reason they instigated a referendum in 2009 to push through the model developed by the citizens' movement. The referendum went their way with an 83.2 percent majority. But the government declared the referendum invalid because the turnout which the government itself had defined as necessary for passing the referendum (40 percent) was not reached; the turnout was only 38.2 percent. Nevertheless, the government promised to pass an improved law, but the drafts for this law gave no indication of any real improvements. For this reason the movement organized yet another referendum, which rejected the state law with a majority of 65.2 percent. A new federal state law is expected in 2015 which will move further in the direction of the citizens' expectations, a true struggle!

Despite this general tendency towards more democracy, many have grave misgivings and apprehensions about direct democracy. Taxes might increase, right-wing populists could stir up hatred against minorities, the death penalty might be reintroduced. The core of such fears is the notion that the general public is not as enlightened and reasonable as an elected government is. The Swiss referendum in 2009 to prevent the construction of new mosque minarets, and also Proposition 8 in California, seems to have confirmed such apprehensions. For this reason I want to discuss the most common misgivings concerning direct democracy and clarify the issue of basic rights using the Swiss referendum on minarets as an example.

Myth no. 1: But we already have representative democracy.

It's an old trick. If someone calls for work breaks or holidays, the response he or she sometimes gets is: "But work is not a bad thing!" Just as breaks and holidays do not call the value of work into question but rather make it more productive, direct democracy does not intend to replace representative democracy but rather to supplement it in meaningful ways. Parliaments may keep their role as regulatory legislators but if they pass a bill that runs contrary to the will of the sovereign people, the latter must have the possibility of correcting its representatives. Or if the platforms of all parties campaigning for seats in parliament lack something that is important to the democratic sovereign, this should have the right to draft a bill itself. And if the electorate chooses a certain government but wishes to change things concerning a certain issue, it should get both of the things they want: the preferred government and the laws of their choice. What matters is that the sovereign people should have the last word.

Myth no. 2: The people can "de-elect" their government.

In the most unfavourable case, this takes four or five years. Governments have a tendency to make unpopular decisions right after they are elected so they can sprinkle more sugar around as the next election approaches. By then much has been forgotten and it would often not even be in the interests of the disappointed voters to stop voting for a political party just because of one or two gross errors if overall they are satisfied with the government's performance. Generally speaking, parliamentary elections are inefficient because the electorate can only choose between large bundles of campaign promises which may or may not be kept, and in the case of coalition governments the blame can also be put on the party's partner. Direct democracy would allow the democratic sovereign to isolate individual issues and decide on them itself. Democracy would become more efficient and satisfactory if the people were not deprived of their right to make decisions between elections but rather had the opportunity to shape society through their own initiative.

Myth no. 3: The people are uneducated.

As a rule, fundamental decisions are ethical decisions and in this respect all human beings are similarly competent – irrespective of their degree of education. There is no indication that society's elite has an above-average measure of nobleness of heart. On the contrary, power corrupts people's characters. A strong intellect alone does not guarantee anything except for the ability to commit crimes in a more subtle fashion. Austria has experienced two referendums: that regarding the Zwentendorf nuclear power plant and that regarding accession to the EU. Concerning one of them, the government and the people had different opinions: on the issue of whether to introduce nuclear power or not. In this controversy, the sovereign people proved to be the more prudent, voting "no", but one of the most aggressive arguments brought forth in this context was that the population "did not understand" the complexities of nuclear science and that such "factual issues" should be clarified by experts. The problem of corrupt expertocracy has been exacerbated in recent years. Ministers and members of parliament would rather listen to lobbyists than to experts with a sense of ethical integrity. Why did thirteen EU governments go to war in Iraq? The "knowledge" argument does not stick.

Myth no. 4: Decisions are too complex.

This argument was implemented in connection with the Treaty of Lisbon of 2009, which amended the founding treaties of the EU. But to begin with, the governments were the ones who created a 500-page monster to keep the democratic sovereigns from having a say by advancing the argument of "complexity" rather than presenting a short and comprehensive constitution. By contrast, the USA gets by fine with a 10-page document (without amendments). Second, surveys showed that most of the representatives of the national parliaments did not have the slightest inkling what the Treaty of Lisbon contained and for this reason they were not the least bit more qualified to vote on it than the general population was.[15] An example from France shows us that referendums actually create a highly informed general public. Books on the EU's constitutional treaty were on the best-seller lists there for months; more than a million copies were sold. In countless public discussions the individual articles of the treaty were debated with fervour into the early hours. If the people are allowed to have a say, they will engage with politics, as the French have proven.

Finally, the most difficult decision of all – the election of a political party – is expected of voters "directly". If the people are presumably too dumb to make prudent decisions, why should they be asked to perform such a feat?

Myth no. 5: This will open the door to rabble-rousing populists.

Rabble-rousing populists are not a speciality of direct democracy. They also campaign in parliamentary elections, and in part they do this so successfully that they get seats in governments. Would this not be a compelling argument against political parties and parliaments? Other methods are required for coping with rabble-rousing populism than the rejection of direct democracy. Here's a hot tip: if governments and parliaments really want to prevent right-wing extremism from gaining in strength, they should finally take measures to combat growing inequality and social division rather than impeding direct democracy.

Myth no. 6: The *Sun* or Fox News would form a de facto government.

This is another killer argument. But it is not an argument against direct democracy (worldwide), but rather an argument in favour of a law that would prevent concentration of media power. Irrespective of this, can one claim that the *Sun* or Fox News has no influence on representative democracy? Once again, the conclusion to be drawn is not that representative democracy should be prevented but rather that the power of the *Sun* and Fox News should be curbed.

Myth no. 7: The death penalty will be reinstated.

And in principle it is right. Theoretically speaking, a majority could vote in favour of the death penalty. Precautions, which I will discuss shortly, would have to be taken to prevent this. But exactly the same holds for indirect democracy, for who is going to protect us against an elected government which reintroduces the death penalty or torture? Guantánamo is not the result of a referendum. The most recent infringements on civil rights and even wars have been the work of parliaments, not citizens! If anything, constitutions and the European Convention on Human Rights safeguard us against violations of human rights. The logical consequence is to see that these ultimate custodians of civil rights also apply for indirect democracy, and not only for direct democracy – which, by the way, is clearly demanded by social movements which advocate for it.

My argument concerning this is that democracy, be it direct or indirect, is only a means. The equality of all human beings, their equal value – human dignity – is the purpose. Equal rights for all derive from the equal value of all human beings, and one of these rights is the right to co-determination. Understandably, the means should never be allowed to eliminate the purpose. Thus all contemporary direct democracy initiatives demand that no previously recognized human rights or minority rights be called into question by direct democracy (or by indirect democracy for that matter), and that democracy itself must not be called into question. Holding a referendum on whether to dissolve parliament and enthrone a king is theoretically conceivable but it should be as impermissible as the installation of a dictator by parliament would be. Minorities may not be repressed by parliament or the people. Human rights either hold for all or they do not hold at all. If they only held for some, democracy would cease to exist because the people would no longer be equal – and this would make every democratic procedure senseless. In such cases the constitution must protect the people's civil rights.

We have arrived at the problem concerning the Swiss ban on the construction of mosque minarets. Switzerland has had a direct democracy since 1848. Accession to the European Human Rights Convention, which the ban on the construction of mosque minarets violates in a twofold sense (in that it violates the ban on discrimination and on freedom of religion), did not occur until 1974. I do not understand how Switzerland can remain a member of the European Human Right Convention. But I am sure that if the Swiss had to decide between revoking the referendum or leaving the European human rights community, a majority of the citizens would vote for equal rights for all, including religious minorities. In countries where direct democracy promises to be introduced in the years to come, the "Minaret Initiative", but also "Proposition 8" in California, should be inadmissible for negating equal rights for everybody. This is, from my point of view, one of the weaknesses of the Californian system: that Proposition 8 was admissable, despite denying such equal rights.[16] Another weakness is that (better) alternatives cannot be added to an approved ballot referendum. According to a poll in 2011, 40 percent of Californians approved the death penalty for murderers, but 48 percent preferred life in prison without parole, instead.[17]

Incidentally, Switzerland abolished the death penalty via direct democracy. If you look at the overall picture you find countless examples which show that the democratic sovereign, when allowed to decide for itself, is more "prudent" than any government. Switzerland has the world's best railway; Austria and Italy have phased out nuclear power; privatization of public utilities was prevented in Leipzig; the Canton of Zurich decided to eliminate tax privileges for wealthy foreigners; Switzerland shortened its compulsive military service and introduced the alternative of a "civilian service". These are all achievements of direct democracy. For this reason people in Switzerland are more satisfied with their political system than the inhabitants of Germany and Austria are with theirs. Some 82 percent of the Austrian population are of the opinion that "the government does not take the interests of the people into account". Only 5 percent believe they have "more say" through elections. Half of the German population thinks that elections give them "no say".[18] In times when governments are co-opted by the economic elite to ever-increasing degrees (Colin Crouch speaks here of "post-democracy",[19] I prefer to call it "pre-democracy"[20]), direct democracy is an urgent imperative. The fact that the sovereign people desires this should be reason enough: 75 percent of those loyal to the CSU/CDU party in Germany are in favour of direct democracy, as are 81 percent of those loyal to the SPD. During the period of French absolutism Louis XIV said: "I am the state!" Today governments and parliaments act in keeping with the slogan "We are the sovereign."

Regarding the EU Lisbon Treaty the representatives of the people who drew it up and enacted it arrogated to themselves the right to decide what or what not the sovereign people were allowed to vote on. If governments and parliaments of the future knew that the sovereign people had the last word, they would take it seriously. And the sovereign citizens would be able to transform their disenchantment with politics and powerlessness into democratic initiative. As Gerald Häfner, a co-founder of the pro-democracy organization Mehr Demokratie e.V. puts it: "Direct democracy means abandoning the stance of the spectator."[21]

SEPARATION OF CONSTITUENT AND CONSTITUTIONAL POWER

The next step is the separation of the power that writes the constitution from the power instituted by it. In political science the attempt is made to distinguish "constituent power" (the sovereign) from "constitutional power" (parliament, government). The idea behind this makes sense; if democratic institutions were allowed to make the rules for governance themselves, they would grant the people as few rights as possible so as to keep most of the power themselves. But if the sovereign people wrote the constitution, it would most probably reserve the right to have the last word as well as the right of co-determination and control.

This point is particularly relevant in the context of the development of the European Union. In the past, basic treaties were always written by governments. The population was excluded from the process of developing new treaties and was also rarely allowed to vote on the final result. This practice is becoming increasingly problematic to the extent that the EU is being assigned new competencies and is slowly being invested with a statelike nature. In addressing the task of drawing up the so-called "EU Constitution", it is high time for the governments to let the sovereign citizens take the helm, for the title "Constitution" indicates the foundation of a sovereign state and the sovereign power of any state must lie in the hands of the population rather than in those of the government or the parliament. The "Constitutional Treaty" was in fact more than a mere constitution; it was a constitution accompanied by political contracts all packed into a monstrous 500-page bundle – a repellent manoeuvre directed against democracy.

After two of the four voting sovereigns (nations) rejected the contractual monster, the governments of EU member states resolved to remove the "constitutional accessories" of the text (for example in the use of the term "laws", a foreign "minister", a flag and a hymn) and to push it through as an "ordinary" treaty. The fact that they simultaneously emphasized having "rescued" 95 percent of the content reveals how an almost identical text was forced upon the sovereigns without them having any right of co-determination whatsoever. Just one single sovereign, the Irish people, voted on this revised document, and the result was a "no" as well. Since, from the perspective of the sovereign's representatives, the results of the vote were not the one desired, another vote was organized. This constituted a further serious abuse of direct democracy . Direct democracy should be an instrument of the sovereign which allows it to correct its government, not an instrument of the government employed to correct the sovereign!

How could an EU treaty come about in a democratic fashion? Seventeen European chapters of the activist organization Attac have made a concrete proposal for how this could be achieved. To build people's trust in the EU and enable them to identify with it, these people would have to be involved in building the "House of Europe". If someone else builds the house and lays down the house rules, this home will not be as cosy for its inhabitants as it would be if they helped decide what it should look like and which rules should apply to it. The proposal made by Attac is as follows: a democratic assembly should be elected, from the population, which is made up of representatives of all member states and consists of at least 50 percent women, whose task would be to write the new basic treaty, whether it is called a constitution or not.[22]

It is customary for such assemblies to be called conventions. The constitutional treaty was in fact written by a convention but this body was not installed by the sovereign people, but by the governments. The convention had no democratic rules of procedure, for the final decision lay with a thirteen-member praesidium rather than with the plenum. The praesidium also "overruled" the plenum when it spoke in favour of holding referendums on the constitutional treaty in all member states. The convention was a farce. Luxembourg's prime minister Jean-Claude Juncker observed: "I have never seen a darkroom that was darker than the convention."[23] No wonder the final product of this darkroom was rejected by three of the five sovereigns who were allowed to vote on it!

According to the proposal made by Attac, the sovereign peoples should have the sole power to decide on the result of the democratic convention. The probability that people would accept a treaty which (a) was written by trusted persons who were elected directly for that express purpose, who (b) maintained a lively exchange of ideas with the people during the editing process and which (c) the sovereign peoples decided on exclusively, is very high. I am convinced that it would be adopted by all the member states, for the central political line of conflict does not run between "national states" or the many diverse European "cultures" but rather between society's elites and the majority of the populations within the many states.

That the final product of a genuinely democratic convention would probably be accepted can be verified elsewhere. In the Canton of Zurich the process described above took place between 1999 and 2005. It entailed direct election of a convention whose task was to write up a new constitution involving intense exchange with the population and voting by the democratic sovereign. The results were accepted with a clear majority of 64.8 percent.[24]

A basic treaty that came about democratically would not only help regain the trust of citizens in the EU; it would put the project of European integration on a substantially different course. I bet that instead of fostering liberties in business, competition between regions, blind freedom in regard to capital transactions, unrestricted property rights, compulsory armament and institutional democratic deficits, a more democratic and a more sustainable and a more peaceful EU would evolve. Much of what is contained in the current treaties would never be written into documents drawn up by the citizens. Instead, civil rights would be given top priority, and these would create a flourishing framework for internal and external peace, and, last but not least, for an Economy for the Common Good.

AN ECONOMIC CONVENTION

Conventions can have the task of writing new constitutions as well as reformulating individual core elements of documents such as the Charter of Fundamental Rights or the framework of values and objectives for business. As I argued before, the current framework of values and objectives and the systemic ground rules (pursuit of profit and competition), which are not constitutional values, not only deviate from our basic human values but are in fact diametrically opposed to them. The economy as it is actually constituted violates the spirit of constitutions. According to the German Basic Law, the "use of property should serve the welfare of the general public", and according to the Constitution of Bavaria, "all business activity serves the common good". The preamble of the US Constitution, meanwhile, recalls that the people of the United States established it "in order to promote the general Welfare". We find little indication of this in business. Constitutional values such as human dignity, solidarity and democracy are demanded in business rarely, if at all. Pursuit of profit and competition are not suitable rules for implementing these basic values.

The proposed democratic economic convention would translate these constitutional values and objectives into ground rules which could lead to successful implementation thereof through effective incentives. The proposals are: to define the pursuit of the common good as the goal of business protagonists, to measure the achievement of this goal in the form of a Common Good Balance Sheet, to measure the success of national economies in the form of a Common Good Product, to promote cooperation between enterprises, to establish ecological rights, and to limit property rights.

Ten to fifteen fundamental ground rules would suffice. The part concerning the economic constitution would probably be three to five pages long. For the first time, ground rules would be set up for business using a democratic procedure.

A CONVENTION ON EDUCATION

Another convention could be established to address issues of education. Through the courses they set, our educational systems decide which human beings will shape future society. Have these people learned how to listen to each other, how to cooperate and respect the opinions of others? Or have they learned to want to be better than others, to use their elbows to get ahead and to disregard everything else for the sake of personal "success"? Are they learning what it means to shape democracy or do they merely view themselves as "private persons"? Do they experience what ultimately holds the world together or are they stuffed full of disjointed bits of knowledge?

There is probably no sector that is more acutely impacted by frustration on all sides than the educational sector. Pupils feel patronized and become aggressive. Teachers feel overwhelmed and abused as scapegoats. Universities are overly regimented and underfinanced. They are increasingly compelled to behave like enterprises so as to procure external funds from profit-oriented private business. External evaluation methods create a climate of surveillance and control. Children and young adults are forced to adapt to the needs of the market and the globalized economy instead of being able to develop into free individuals with a critical mindset.

Does this development comply with the ideal of free education? Why are pupils and parents not allowed to help define curricula? Why does the government reserve the right to do this? Is this not a matter that affects everyone? Are not those members of society who are affected by education more intelligent in sum than a government that is beleaguered by interest groups?

A democratic convention for education with trusted delegates elected from all areas affected by it – pupils, students, teachers, parents – which defined the goals and core learning contents of the educational system as well as determining rights of co-determination for those involved would offer a way out of the dilemma. I wager that the learning content and the curricula they chose would differ substantially from what the head of Austria's conservative party and Vice Chancellor Josef Pröll proposed in 2009 in his programmatic speech entitled "Project Austria" at the height of the financial crisis. His proposal was that "financial education" should become a "component of every type of school education".[25] Or, now that the banks have become global casinos, the entire population should learn how to have the greatest possible success playing at its gambling tables. The fact that the only representative sent by Austria to the EU Commission's task group of the same name (namely "Financial Education") is the managing director of the hedge funds firm Superfund, which lures its clients with financial returns of 20 to 70 percent annually, says it all.[26] (The two German members come from the banking association and the association of insurers respectively.)[27]

A PUBLIC SERVICES CONVENTION

A third convention could define the area of cost-efficient public services. The crucial question is: Which sectors of business are so essential (and in many cases most easily organized in the form of uniform operation) that they should be put under the complete control of the sovereign people? According to surveys, a large majority of the European population is in favour of a public postal service, a public railway system, a publicly funded pension system, public health insurance and public kindergartens and universities. These public service operations could be developed into "democratic commons" via a public services convention. (In cases where the population has been given the opportunity to vote, they have spoken out in favour of maintaining public control over basic infrastructures.)

A MEDIA CONVENTION

Another convention could address issues of the media so as to de-merge the power of the media, business and politics with an aim towards cultivating a more democratic media environment. Diversity and deconcentration of power could make for negative feedback in this area as well:

- no enterprise would be permitted to own part of more than one media company;
- no media company would be dependent on any one advertiser for more than 0.5 percent of its expenditures on advertising;
- new media with a start-up budget exceeding a defined threshold could only be founded by at least five accredited journalists and at least ten equally large owners.

No government would even dream of distributing media and property power. The only entity that would tackle and implement this rescue measure for democracy would be the democratic sovereign. But direct democracy would be needed to do this.

A DEMOCRACY CONVENTION

Since the crisis in 2008 and the reaction of governments to this crisis (or the lack of reaction), more and more people are realizing that the current model of democracy is actually a dead-end street. Many civil society initiatives, ranging from the Occupy movement to Attac, from the Initiative and Referendum Institute to Democracy International, are putting thought to how democracy can be advanced, or rather how *democracia real*, as it is called by the Spanish Indignados movement, could be achieved in the first place. In my opinion this is one of the largest tasks facing us over the coming years. All forces that desire more democracy will have to join together to work out an innovative model of democracy in keeping with the times and then strive to make this the common demand of a wide-scale civic alliance, which is to say, a civil rights movement that would really make history.

The path to implementation could be a popular initiative, the demand for a democracy convention, or, in this case, even a party. I personally tend to think that parties are a dead end on the way to "genuine" democracy because they emphasize the factional rather than the mutual. What factions propose is rejected by other factions out of principle – not for substantive reasons. Party democracy calls for competition, but democracy should be based on cooperative procedures. I am not able to offer any well-honed solution here, but I suspect that processes will soon be found for satisfying the needs of the community and making sustainable decisions without the body politic being split up and wearing itself down as a result.

The democracy party, should one ever exist, would have one sole aim, namely to give birth to the new model of democracy. Its platform would address no substantive issues – no matter how much majority appeal these might have – for these would distract too much from the task of formulating new ground rules for decision-making processes. Moreover, proposals that were capable of winning a majority could be written into law after implementation of the new rules – and with no party participation.

The search for a better model of democracy has begun. I believe it will be the most important political project of the years to come.

A THREE-PILLAR DEMOCRACY

In total the proposed measures would enable the current one-dimensional model of democracy (which is solely representative) to evolve into a three-dimensional democracy: an indirect democracy (representative), a direct democracy (involving conventions and referendums) and a participative democracy (involving co-determination in business and public services). What it would ultimately achieve is a better division of labour among those holding political power and those to whom – in part – such power was to be delegated. That would still not constitute any "genuine democracy", dear Jean-Jacques Rousseau, but it would at least be a first step in this direction.

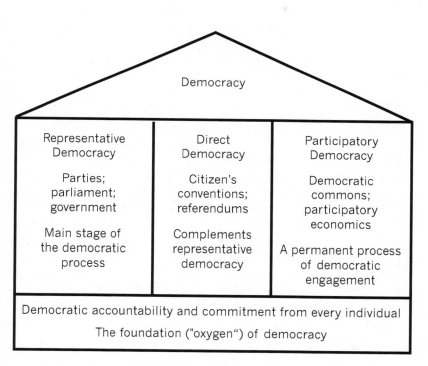

Evolution of Democracy

SEVEN
REAL WORLD EXAMPLES

The Economy for the Common Good is not a utopia. Enterprises have always pursued goals other than profit gain. And cooperation is a basic principle not only of evolution,[1] but also of numerous alternative forms of business which have been practised prior to, alongside and beyond capitalism. More people work full-time in the cooperatives of the world than in all the transnational corporations put together.[2] Banking cooperatives modelled on the one developed by Friedrich Wilhelm Raiffeisen exist in 180 countries across the globe. Commons include everything from alpine pastures and drinking water cooperatives to free software and internet applications. Notions like circulation economy, blue economy, shared value and public value point to numerous alternatives, all of which are committed to the same values. What all have in common is that they view money and capital as mere means, whereas the goals they set are of a higher and more diverse nature.

Within the private business sector thousands of enterprises already exist – amidst global capitalism – that comply with most aspects of the Economy for the Common Good. The Economy for the Common Good wants to make these practices visible and reward them. The following examples testify to the existence of such practices, and of course they also stand for many other models. Together they exert an inspirational and motivating effect on many people and there are no reasonable grounds for not striving to shape a full-scale entrepreneurial environment according to their collective example.

I. MONDRAGÓN – THE WORLD'S LARGEST COOPERATIVE (IN THE BASQUE REGION OF SPAIN)

The Basque Mondragón Corporación Cooperativa (MCC) is currently the world's largest cooperative. In 1943, after the end of the Spanish Civil War, a young priest named José María Arizmendiarrieta established a polytechnic vocational school. In 1956 five graduates of this school founded the first cooperative. Today the group is represented in nineteen countries comprising 256 enterprises in the sectors of mechanical engineering, the automotive industry, the construction industry, household appliances, retail trade, finance and insurance companies. They also have their own cooperative bank, the Caja Laboral Popular.

83 percent of the approximately 75,000 employees are members of the cooperative. The aim is to increase this proportion to 90 percent. The cooperative is based on the principle that all of its employed members are fundamentally equal. The democratic company organization is reflected in (a) the sovereignty of the general assembly, which is made up of all members of the cooperative and which operates on the principle of "one person, one vote"; (b) democratic election of members of management bodies, in particular the supervisory board, which reports to the general assembly; and (c) collaboration with the executive organs, which are set up to manage the cooperative on the instructions of the members of the cooperative as a whole.

A small portion of the profits are paid out to the employees but the largest part is reinvested. Another part of the profits flows into the Central Fund for Cooperation, which implements new projects and creates new jobs. If a business finds itself in financial difficulties, the losses can be absorbed through wage cuts if these are approved by the employees. In the event of serious financial problems or order peaks, employees work in other cooperatives for short periods of time. Up to 10 percent of the net profit goes to the community and is invested in education projects, which are given very high priority. After all, this is how it all began. The Mondragón Group has an overall turnover of 15 billion euros; its equity capital amounts to 5 billion euros. The degree of globalization is high; subsidiaries are to be found everywhere from Portugal to Thailand, Brazil to Poland, and Mexico to Hong Kong.

Here are some of the enterprise's self-declared (open) secrets of success:

- Not profit, but human beings take centre stage here. Co-property and co-determination of all are an expression of this philosophy. Some 45 percent of the employees are women.
- Reinvestment of practically all earned revenue. (There are no shareholders.)
- Creation of effective instruments of mutual cooperation; at Mondragón people are not even laid off in times of crisis – although this has changed since the 2008 crisis. Profits saved up in the solidarity fund are used to strengthen floundering operations in the group. In addition the cooperative bank grants loans to prospering cooperatives at higher interest rates while asking very low interest rates or no interest at all from cooperatives that find themselves in a difficult situation.

The last point shows how systematic cooperation between enterprises could work. At Mondragón this basic principle of the Economy for the Common Good is already an established practice. For David Schweickart, a professor of philosophy from Chicago, Mondragón was the source of inspiration for developing an alternative business model which he calls "economic democracy".[3] As Karl Marx wrote, "[Men's] social being ... determines their consciousness."[4]

2. SEKEM – ORGANIC FARMING IN THE DESERT (EGYPT)

Sekem is an Egyptian fair-trade cooperative 60 kilometres south of Cairo which was founded in 1977 and has now evolved into seven enterprises with a total of 1,850 employees.[5] Sekem brought organic farming to the desert and made it thrive there, producing organic foods and health products along with ecological textiles. Sekem means "vital energy from the sun". Founder Ibrahim Abouleish was awarded the Alternative Nobel Prize in 2003 for his "business model for the 21st century which integrated business success and the social and cultural development of society through an economy of love".

One of the seven enterprises is the phytopharmaceutical enterprise Atos, which produces natural remedies for the treatment of cancer, cardiovascular diseases, skin diseases and rheumatism; Isis produces organic grains, rice, vegetables, noodles, honey, jams, dates, herbs, spices, teas and fruit juices; Libra is an organic farm operation which has developed biodynamic processes for producing cotton, oilseeds and grain on cooperative farms all over Egypt; Lotus dries herbs; Hator markets fresh fruits; Mizan reproduces seeds for vegetable farmers; and Conytex-Naturetex manufactures ecological textiles. Research for all the enterprises is conducted at the interdisciplinary Sekem Academy for Applied Art and Science.

In addition to biodynamic agriculture, another focus of the enterprise is fair trade. In the beginning the fair-trade principle was restricted to trade with industrial countries, but now Sekem is attempting to establish this principle in Egypt's domestic market as well. The third focus is the well-being of the group's 1,850 employees. Kindergartens,

Steiner schools and clinics are funded from their earnings. A free university opened its gates in September 2009.

The employees from all enterprises gather together every morning to express appreciation for the work of the previous day and to greet the new one. The cooperative's central values – human dignity, equality and democracy – are cultivated by the Sekem employees. Its educational institutions are committed to promoting "free and clear thinking" as well as "artistic expression". The health centres work on the basis of holistic and natural medicine.

The Abouleish Foundation holds Sekem's capital; the foundation council oversees the vision of the cooperative. In February 2007 the GLS Community Bank of Frankfurt and the Tridos Bank acquired a 20 percent stake in the Sekem Group.

3. GÖTTIN DES GLÜCKS ("GODDESS OF FORTUNE") AND CRAFT AID – ECO-FAIR TEXTILES (MAURITIUS/AUSTRIA)

Göttin des Glücks (GDG) is the first Austrian eco-fair trade textile label. It was founded in 2005 by four artists from Bulgaria, Croatia and Austria.[6] The aim of this fashion enterprise is to make everyone happy: manufacturers, customers and the Earth. The clothing is sewn by Craft Aid (CA), a trade partner of EZA Fairer Handel, on Mauritius. As a long-term cooperation partner of EZA, Göttin des Glücks can make use of a continuous, certified eco-fair production chain; it's a win–win situation for all. CA is a fair-trade-certified, non-profit enterprise which was founded in 1982 to help reintegrate disabled persons into society by giving them employment. Today CA has 180 employees who work in the sugar, flowers and clothing sectors, half of whom are people with special needs. All employees are picked up at their homes in the morning and brought back after they finish work. The nine-hour work day is interrupted by three breaks, which are conscientiously observed.

There is no overtime; the employees earn 1.5 times the customary pay for those working in the textile industry on Mauritius. All employees have health and accident insurance, and in addition each employee has a savings book into which pension contributions are paid. Every Monday the firm is visited by a doctor who offers medical examinations free of charge. In addition to freedom of expression all employees are given the opportunity to make suggestions for ways to improve the enterprise.

Profits are donated for charitable purposes and invested in expanding the enterprise. Something the company is particularly proud of is the GOTS (Global Organic Textile Standard) certification which it received in 2010 with the support of EZA. This is currently the highest-level global textile eco seal in existence for this production chain.

4. FAIR TRADE – APPRECIATING THE PEOPLE BEHIND THE PRODUCTS (58 PRODUCING COUNTRIES)

Fair trade sets a counterpoint to "free trade" and the "low-cost supplier" principle. It was designed to give those beaten down by the system – small farmers, artisans and textile workers – a chance on the world market. Adequate prices for their products along with reliable and preferably direct trade relations strengthen their position on the market vis-à-vis global players and provide an important basis for improving their life situation. Observance of social and ecological criteria plays a major role for cultivation of products and working conditions.

In Europe, Worldshops – retail shops for fair-trade products – have contributed to propagating the fair-trade concept. Apart from serving as sales points they provide information, raise awareness and facilitate encounters with people from the products' countries of origin. Many Worldshops employ volunteers; if human beings were so self-serving and competitive "by nature", as some claim they are, these shops would all have to close down.

With the creation of the FAIRTRADE label (founded in the Netherlands in 1988), commercial market players too, such as supermarkets, have gained controlled access to the concept of fair trade. Since then, sales and the product range have grown. Global sales of FAIRTRADE-certified products amounted to some 3.4 billion euros in the year 2009. Despite this, there has been some criticism of FAIRTRADE in recent years, and the audit and certification process must be put on a transparent and independent basis in response to this.[7]

In the Economy for the Common Good, products traded on a fair basis would be granted privileged status over those traded in unfair ways until, after a transition period of several years, products produced and traded on a fair basis would become the only ones found on the shelves of shops and stores. This could be achieved by a progressive mark-up for custom duties on unfairly traded products, for example; then the fairly traded products would soon become less expensive. The World Trade Organization, which fosters competition and dumping prices, might declare "discrimination" of unfairly traded products to be illegal, viewing it as a violation of free trade laws, but this would be just another reason for rescinding free trade laws and instead asserting fair and equitable trade regulations in the UN.[8] After all, protection of human rights, labour laws and the environment cannot be voluntary.

5. SEMCO – "INDUSTRIAL DEMOCRACY" (BRAZIL)

SEMCO[9] was founded in Brazil in the 1950s, It originally manufactured centrifuges for the plant oil industry. Today it is active on the world market for business services: environmental consultancy, property management, real estate consulting, office equipment, and steering wheels. In the areas of industrial equipment, postal services and document administration, the enterprise with over 3,000 employees is a market leader.

What is remarkable about SEMCO is its alternative organizational model. Hierarchies and pre-defined company organograms do not exist in the customary form. No value is placed on formalities; instead, priorities lie in mutual respect, co-determination and co-participation. All employees are treated equally irrespective of their task, or whether they have a managerial or an executive function. Every task is invested with meaning, which makes everyone more motivated and content.

When Ricardo Semler, the son of the founder Antonio Curt Semler, took charge of managing the business in the 1980s, he encountered financial difficulties so he decided to implement extensive restructuring measures. The former key objective had been to increase the business's performance and production indices. Later the focus was placed on social factors such as the well-being and motivation of its employees. The basic conviction shared by all is based on a dynamic model. Participation of employees has a positive effect on their motivation, and this in turn increases participation.

Embracing this approach, the "persons" at SEMCO (as employees are called there) developed a new organization chart. Flexible working hours were introduced in all work units. A rotation model was adopted in various work units as well, which made for more variety and enabled the business to replace any absent employees. The employees themselves decide how much holiday time they get, and when, as well as how much they earn, these issues being negotiated on a transparent, decentralized basis.

In the "Survival Manual" (Manual de Sobrevivência), ground rules for working together at SEMCO are laid down. Every individual who joins SEMCO is encouraged to participate, scrutinize goals and processes and be creative.

In keeping with the company's entrepreneurial culture, any person who wants to take on a managerial position must be accepted by the employees he or she is to be "in charge of". Putting pressure on employees, issuing threats or creating stress are viewed as managerial deficits. Terms such as "employee" and "co-worker" are avoided. The business prefers to use the word "person" as the central concept for all those working for SEMCO. Mutual respect replaces formalities. The climate is open for freedom of expression concerning ideas and criticism. Differences of opinion are viewed as necessary and healthy.

This form of industrial democracy increases the self-reliance of all persons involved. The profits and results of each working unit are transparent and accessible to all. Some 15 percent of the profits are paid out to the workers. Use of a balance sheet rate allows everyone to participate in the discussion as to how profits should be used.

The SEMCO model has stood the test. An enterprise that once faced bankruptcy is now a profitable group with twelve business divisions. SEMCO is one of the best workplaces in Brazil and in the area of human resources.[10]

Ricardo Semler was named Latin-American Businessman of the Year by the *Wall Street Journal* in 1990, and in 1992 he was named Brazilian Businessman of the Year. His first book, *Turning the Tables*, is the best-selling non-fiction title in Brazil's history, and has been translated into twenty-three languages.[11]

6. COMMUNITY-SUPPORTED AGRICULTURE (USA AND WORLDWIDE)

The practice of "community supported agriculture" (CSA), inspired by the biodynamic agriculture of Rudolf Steiner, started in 1986 in two US farms: the CSA Garden at Great Barrington (Massachusetts) and the Temple-Wilton Community Farm in New Hampshire.[12] Its concept is as simple as it is ingenious: farms supply the region with foodstuffs and the region provides farms with the financial means it needs to operate. The consumers take responsibility for the production of organic foods by giving a purchase guarantee for example for a year. In return they are informed on production processes and exert influence on them. They become a part of the business organism. This concept is rooted in the idea that within certain healthy cycles, nature produces enough surplus to nourish the people of the region.[13] In the 1980s, CSA spread throughout many regions of North America – mainly in New England and the Northwest, on the Pacific Coast, in the Upper Midwest and Canada. In 2007, the US census of agriculture counted almost 13,000 CSA farms. California was in the lead with almost 1,000 practitioners.[14] In Germany, the Buschberghof Demeter farm is viewed as the nucleus of all community-supported farms in the country.[15] Since 1987, the farm has strived to implement a closed economic cycle which involves in the production process not only the agricultural businesses but also the consumers. Other outstanding examples are the Kattendorfer Hof and the CSA Hof Pente. In Austria, the Ochsenherz Gärtnerhof works together with 200 harvest shareholders. The principle of mutual responsibility for organic and regional–seasonal production is also implemented in food coops and box schemes. The CSA farms network in the UK was launched in late 2013.[16]

7. REGIONALWERT AG – REGIONAL EQUITY CAPITAL (GERMANY)

In 2006 the citizen share company Regionalwert AG was founded near Freiburg, Germany.[17] The five hundred or so shareholders make it possible for sustainable regional agricultural businesses to be financed. At the time of writing 1.97 million euros have been raised. The capital made available in this way is used by Regionalwert AG to buy agricultural and related businesses, which are in turn leased to financially weak entrepreneurs. Financial investments are made in newly set-up businesses along the entire value-added chain: training, plant breeding, agrarian production (cultivation of land, livestock farming, market gardening, silviculture), processing (dairying, cheese making, bakeries ...) and sales (retailing, catering, gastronomy ...). As a form of extra-financial "profit" the shareholders receive "multi-dimensional wealth" and added "socio-ecological value" calculated by means of certain indicators, along with security of supply in the region.

8. ETHICAL BANKS IN GERMANY, SWITZERLAND, ITALY, THE NETHERLANDS AND AUSTRIA

Today some banks have already pledged themselves to serve the common good. The German Gemeinschaftsbank für Leihen und Schenken (GLS)[18] is a cooperative bank which was founded by anthroposophists in 1974. It is the first universal bank in Germany that operates according to socio-ecological principles. It finances over 6,500 enterprises and projects in the areas of free schools and nurseries, regenerative energy, institutions for the disabled, residences, sustainable building, and life in old age. Loans are not granted to companies that produce things such as alcohol, nuclear energy, weapons or tobacco or to those that engage in green gene technology, or in animal experiments, or that use child labour. All loans granted to enterprises are publicized in the customer magazine *Bankspiegel*. On principle, no loans are resold, nor does the bank engage in any speculative transactions. In 2013, the bank deposits of the customers amounted to 2.8 billion euros. The GLS Trust is a part of the bank; it administers foundations and awards money to non-profit projects. In addition to the bank's main office in Bochum, there are six branches which employ a total of 450 people.

The first alternative bank in Switzerland, which was also founded by anthroposophic circles, is the Freie Gemeinschaftsbank.[19] It started out in Dornach in 1984, moving to Basel in 1999. Its objective is to support non-profit projects and other initiatives which aim to serve the general public by granting loans according to ethical criteria. Emphasis is put on certified organic farms, free schools, kindergartens, training institutions, curative education and social therapy, physicians' practices, clinics, therapeutics, trade, commerce, restaurants, ecological projects, regenerative energies, art schools, artistic initiatives, nursing homes and community living. The bank's total assets amount to some 200 million Swiss francs and it has equity capital amounting to some 8 million Swiss francs. The share certificates of the cooperative are not paid back, nor do they bear interest.

Another ethical bank in Switzerland is the Alternative Bank Schweiz (ABS) with headquarters in Olten, which was founded in 1990 by 2,600 individuals and enterprises. Today it boasts total assets of almost one billion euros.[20] The ABS also grants loans focused on alternative projects. Another trademark of the ABS is its transparency; it publishes the names of borrowers and states the purpose of loans granted to them. Democracy and equal opportunities for women and men play an important role in the business. The bank has 24,000 customers and 4,400 shareholders.

At the Sparda Banks in Germany and Austria, all account holders are simultaneously members of the cooperative and thus co-owners who are entitled to vote. The Sparda Bank Munich, an exemplary bank among the Sparda Banks, has 224,000 owners.[21] They elect over 200 representatives and, in turn, these elect the supervisory and executive boards. The representatives decide how profits should be distributed. Over the past few years, real dividends on cooperative capital usually amounted to around five to six percent. The wage differential for members of the executive board and employees with average earnings was 6 to 1. For the 660 employees some 120 different working time models exist. The standard working time – 37.75 hours per week – lies below the collective wage agreement. Parents of children between the age of one and three receive a childcare allowance of 150 euros a month. In 2010 Sparda Banks was awarded the prize for "Germany's Best Employer" in the category of banks for the fourth time. In the

"Kundenmonitor Deutschland" (a German customer survey), the group of Sparda Banks ranked first for the seventeenth time. The bank's assets now exceed 5 billion euros.

In 1999, Banca Etica was founded in Padova. It is the first Italian bank entirely dedicated to ethical finance,[22] and has more than 37,000 members who hold 46 million euros in share capital. In its first fifteen years, Banca Etica has provided more than 23,000 loans to families and social enterprises in all 20 Italian regions. Some 70 percent of its loans have gone to non-profit organizations, one third to social enterprises. The staff comprises two hundred employees. Banca Etica has another merit: it initiated the foundation of FEBEA, the Europen Federation of Ethical and Alternative Banks and Financiers.[23] On the global level, ethical banks have built the Global Alliance for Banking on Values.[24] Both associations could serve as the starting point for an official European banking federation for the common good that enjoys a less rigid degree of regulation than for-profit and investment banks.

Oikocredit is an international credit organization founded in 1975 which specializes in micro and project loans in connection with development assistance. Some 797 loan projects are supported in 71 countries worldwide. The capital, which benefits a total of 17.5 million people, is provided by 34,000 investors and organizations from fifteen countries. The organization is headquartered in the Netherlands. The Society for the Promotion of Oikocredit Austria was founded in 1990; Austria's contribution of over 1,950 investors currently has assets amounting to almost 20 million euros.[25]

9. JOHN LEWIS – A ROLE MODEL FOR EMPLOYEE OWNERSHIP (UK)

The John Lewis Partnership is the largest employee-owned company in the UK. The partnership's 69,000 partners own the leading UK retail businesses Waitrose, John Lewis and Greenbee. All permanent employees are partners. In all, 43 John Lewis shops, 332 Waitrose supermarkets, an online and catalogue business and other business units turned over a total of almost £7 billion in 2013. The partnership's three strategic goals are providing advantages for the partners such as happiness and community, realization of market potential through use of a sustainability strategy, and "peace of mind about product sourcing".

John Lewis Partnership shares are held in trust. The beneficiaries of this trust are the employees of the company. They share the profit and oversee management decisions by means of a number of democratic bodies. A very characteristic feature of the company is its "Constitution", which lays down its principles, governance system and rules. Founder John Spedan Lewis, who signed away his personal ownership rights, wanted to leave some clear guidelines for his successors so that the values that had motivated him would not be eroded with the passage of time. Lewis aimed for a "better form of business", that is, one which is not driven by the demands of outside shareholders and which sets high standards of behaviour in many realms. Thanks to this spirit, the project has managed to maintain and even improve its competitiveness relative to conventional retailers.[26]

10. GEA, GUGLER*, SONNENTOR, THOMA, ZOTTER – PIONEERS IN VARIOUS BRANCHES (AUSTRIA)

GEA with its legendary "Waldviertler" (a type of shoe) is an example of how one can fly in the face of globalization, location shifting and cheap production by manufacturing traditional consumer goods using local resources and a regional workforce, and coupling production and sales. At the Waldviertler GmbH and the GEA Heinrich Staudinger GmbH a total of 125 people manufacture shoes and furniture. The minimum monthly net pay is just under one thousand euros; the maximum salary ratio between top and bottom earners is 2:1. Since the autumn of 2010 the production sites at Waldviertel have produced more electricity by means of their own solar collectors than they can use themselves.

gugler*, a communications service provider in the Lower Austrian city of Melk, has a vision – making print products completely compostable. They subscribe to the Cradle to Cradle® principle, which could be adopted as one of the "supreme goals" on the Economy for the Common Good Balance Sheet.[27] For more than twenty years this family business (with 95 employees) has been taking innovative steps to make media production eco-friendly. Awards such as the Lower Austrian Wood Timber Frame Construction Prize 2000, the Trigos 2004, the WWF Panda Award 2006 and the Austrian Sustainability Reporting Award 2008 all confirm their comprehensive commitment. This is also laid out in the long-term entrepreneurial strategy: "business conduct mindful of the welfare of human beings and the Earth".

The organic herb processer Sonnentor of Lower Austria, which was founded in 1988, also is exploring ways to promote social and ecological sustainability.[28] It too looks back on a long list of relevant prizes and awards such as the Neighbouring Business award for the southwestern part of Lower Austria. Some 153 employees process natural products from 150 farms in the region, exporting them to almost fifty countries. The range of products includes teas, herbs, salt, coffee and more. The business uses 100 percent recyclable or compostable packaging materials and exclusively green electricity; one tenth of their power demand is covered by a photovoltaic installation. No direct emissions are generated at the business location. Together with the other three aforementioned enterprises and several more such as Rogner Bad Blumau and the Fandler oil mill, Sonnentor has co-authored the Blumauer Manifest, which espouses entrepreneurial responsibility and sustainability.[29]

At Goldegg of Salzburg, Erwin *Thoma* has built a business which produces timber houses made entirely without the use of glue or metal. These so-called Holz100 houses are already to be found in 25 countries all over the globe. The wood used by the enterprise is the first to have been awarded Cradle to Cradle Gold certification.

Riegersburg in Styria, Austria, is the home of Europe's only 100 percent organic fair-trade chocolate factory, which processes 250 tons of cocoa beans from Nicaragua, Peru, the Dominican Republic, Ecuador, Costa Rica, Panama, Bolivia and Brazil annually. Founder Josef Zotter is joined by one hundred employees who carry out all production steps "from bean to bar" – roasting, rolling and conching – at one site. Since 2004 only fair-trade beans and sugar have been used, and since 2006 all ingredients have been organic. Making chocolate does not necessarily entail child labour or mass husbandry.[30]

II. CECOSESOLA – A MULTI-COOPERATIVE (VENEZUELA)

In the Venezuelan metropolis of Barquisimeto the employees of an undertaker and bus enterprise took over the business after it went bankrupt and converted it into a cooperative, eliminating its hierarchical structures and putting decision-making processes on a consensus basis. Four supermarkets form the core of the cooperative; they are open from Friday to Sunday and serve as meeting places and cultural centres. Their appeal lies in their fresh, high-quality goods. Numerous farmers and gardeners deliver goods to the cooperative directly. The wages are 50 percent above the Venezuelan minimum wage (which is already relatively high for Latin America) and the prices are consumer-oriented. Ninety-nine percent of the tasks are performed according to the rotation principle: employees alternate their roles in achieving them. In addition to the supermarkets there is a health centre for which more than US$ 2million has already been raised, with the money coming from the company's own resources, donations and solidarity events. The buildings are finished. What is missing now is the expensive medical equipment. The government has offered to pay for this but the cooperative has rejected the offer so as to preserve its independence. A collective bank is also being set up which will help finance the health centre. Cecosesola has about 2,000 direct employees and 50,000 members. The supermarkets are the largest in the entire city, and the undertaker business carries out some ninety burials monthly.

12. A SOLIDARITY-BASED ECONOMY (BRAZIL)

In Brazil an alternative business sector is growing: the solidarity-based economy. It emerged in response to the crisis of capitalism in the 1980s, during which unprecedented mass unemployment prevailed, threatening to throw many people into abject poverty. With the free market incapable of helping them, they looked to self-help and solidarity instead. Numerous cooperatives evolved. Today, more than 20,000 businesses exist which have an overall headcount of over 2 million. The spectrum of businesses ranges from sugar and shoe factories to seamstresses' cooperatives to fair-trade networks. Some businesses are self-run production enterprises, some are agrarian cooperatives, and some are informal networks established in poor quarters and indigenous communities. Five hundred organizations and eighty cities have supported the establishment of the solidarity-based economic sector. The state secretary in charge, Paul Singer, holds the view that whereas capitalism encourages people to embrace egoism and greed, the solidarity-based economy has just as great an impact in promoting solidarity and a Common Good orientation. Students who do practical training in solidarity-based businesses are eager to stay there, he reports, adding that mutual assistance is the backbone of this fragile sector. The first profits made by a sugar factory run by employees themselves did not end up in the pockets of anonymous shareholders but rather went to educating the employees and helping them overcome their illiteracy.

13. OPEN SOURCE (GLOBAL)

The Economy for the Common Good relies on knowledge being passed on, not on it being isolated to serve commercial interests. That this does not contradict human nature is illustrated by the history of science, which consists of systemic cooperation; insights gathered and published by the individual are immediately put at the disposal of all future researchers. In the high-tech sector a branch of industry exists which embraces this principle: the open-source and free-software movement. Activists in this area agree that private firms should not be permitted to patent computer software, application programmes and operating systems, but that such products should be continuously developed in an "open", cooperative fashion. This spirit has given birth to a series of free high-tech products ranging from the Linux operating system and the Firefox web browser to the Thunderbird mail programme and the online encyclopedia Wikipedia. Whoever discovers something has the honour of seeing his or her contribution become part of a grander scheme. This is a basic human need; we all want to make a meaningful contribution, and are glad to do so without profiting from it.

14. "NON-PROFIT" – 170,000 WORKPLACES IN NON-PROFIT ORGANIZATIONS (AUSTRIA)

Despite stock exchange fever, despite the lure of 25 percent returns on investment, and despite a flood of glossy business magazines, non-profit organizations (NPOs) are nevertheless part of daily life. According to statistics published by Johns Hopkins University, which has been gathering figures on the NPO sector in the forty largest countries of the world for the past fifteen years, NPOs currently employ 31 million people, 20 million of whom are paid employees. These NPOs boast revenues of more than US$1.3 trillion – half the economic output of Germany – annually.[31] In the USA, the non-profit sector contributed an estimated $887 billion to the economy in 2012, comprising 5.4 percent of the country's GDP.[32] The sector consists of 1.44 million public charities, private foundations and other types of non-profit organization, including chambers of commerce, fraternal organizations and civic leagues. Together, they accounted for 9.2 percent of all wages and salaries in the USA.[33] In the UK, the non-profit sector provides 800,000 jobs, two thirds of them full-time. More than 160,000 organizations in the most diverse areas – from education and culture to environment and village halls bodies – had a combined income of £39 billion in 2012.[34] In Austria just under 2 percent of the added value – some 5 billion euros – is earned in non-profit-oriented places of employment. Thus the non-profit sector is larger than each of the following sectors: agriculture and forestry, fisheries, the food and beverage industry, the tobacco industry, the paper and cardboard industry, the printing and publishing sector, or the vehicle manufacture industry. Some 40 percent of the 171,000 workplaces are paid full-time.

These numerous examples contradict the widespread misconception that enterprises which do not pursue profit would not make sense and would not function properly.

15. SATISFACTION OF NEEDS AND VOLUNTEER WORK AT NO COST (ANYWHERE, ANYTIME)

It is possible to create meaningful added value not only without pursuit of profit, but also without money. Many essential needs must be met in our capitalist environment outside the arena of markets and money. In fact, on the "free" market many basic needs are ignored (a billion human beings are starving although the planet provides sufficient food for all). At the same time, people go to great lengths to meet artificially generated needs and even addictions.

The capitalist economy treats unpaid, voluntary services, in particular the extremely valuable work provided by women in the home, as a matter of course. Such services include child care, nursing care, elderly care and end-of-life care. It thus seems particularly cynical when people claim human beings would not perform at all without being driven by competition and the pursuit of profit. Let us remind ourselves of some of these "invisible achievements" which capitalism relies on:

- Mother's milk is not charged for, and nor are pregnancies or years of childcare.
- Patient care: when the ill are nursed to health by their partners, they pay nothing.
- Care of the elderly is most often provided by women, often for no pay.
- End-of-life (hospice) care is done primarily on a volunteer basis.
- Care of the homeless and drug addicts; food distribution to the needy.
- In Austria, if someone has a car accident, they are often brought to hospital by volunteer rescuers. If this person has lost blood, they will probably receive some from a completely unknown donor. Not only milk, but also blood is free of charge.
- If someone must quickly do research for a presentation they might consult Wikipedia, making use of knowledge put at their disposal by people from all over the world. And to do so they might use Firefox as an internet browser, which is completely free of charge and corporate influence. It might even be that their enterprise decides to switch over to Linux, the no-cost operating system. These days even high-tech is sometimes free of charge.

In 2010, 63 million Americans, almost 20 percent of the population, volunteered in the non-profit sector. Their work was valued at $284 billion at average private wages.[35] In the UK, 27 percent of the population volunteers on a regular (monthly) basis, while 44 percent volunteer at least once a year.[36] In Germany, 34 percent of the population works on a volunteer basis a total of 4.6 billion work hours annually – as much as the working hours clocked up by 3.2 million full-time employees.[37]

The principle of donation and benevolence (Adam Smith) is universal and ineradicable even in capitalistic societies. The approach of the "gift economy" proposes extending this principle to the entire economy.[38] Perhaps this is the second step to take. The first step would be to renounce making money as the supreme purpose of business and work, replacing it with quality of life, nurture, creativity and the common good.

EIGHT
PUTTING IT INTO PRACTICE

You never change things by fighting the
existing reality. To change something, build a new
model that makes the existing model obsolete.
Buckminster Fuller

The movement for an Economy for the Common Good began on
6 October 2010. The first fifteen enterprises – run by Attac businesspeople
– which worked together with me in developing the first version of
this book, organized a conference entitled "Rethinking Enterprise" in
Vienna. Instead of the anticipated fifty or so guests, over a hundred
people showed up, two thirds of whom were entrepreneurs. They got
down to work immediately. Numerous work groups were set up around
a bunch of pioneer companies, forming the nucleus of a highly complex
organizational structure which has taken shape in subsequent years. This
structure is an important part of the strategy: individuals from diverse
realms of society contribute their skills and expertise to help create the
Economy for the Common Good. The strategy includes various tasks:
pioneering enterprises draw up a Common Good Balance Sheet on

a voluntary basis; business consultants support pioneers in this initial process; auditors approve the Common Good Balance Sheets; editors continuously revise the template for the Common Good Balance Sheet based on feedback received; universities incorporate the Economy for the Common Good model into their curricula and conduct research into it; speakers spread the idea all over the globe; ambassadors circulate it in regional associations and political parties, and local chapters (also known as "energy fields") pave the way for the change to come at local levels. The first Association for the Promotion of the Economy for the Common Good was founded in July 2011. By late 2014, an additional fifteen associations had been established at the local and national levels in Italy, Switzerland, Germany, Spain and Argentina. In the meantime, economic pioneers have been joined by political and cultural trailblazers. All these elements have evolved naturally, without any master plan. The first strategy was not developed until the autopoietic "ecosystem" for the Economy for the Common Good had already taken shape.[1] Now, four years after its inception, the structure of the international movement can be represented on four levels:

1. **Pioneer groups:** enterprises and organizations (business), municipalities and regions (politics), as well as schools and universities (education) begin implementing the ideas.
2. **Substantive level:** expert teams such as editors, consultants, auditors, speakers, ambassadors, municipal facilitators and mediators advance the idea, designing processes and supporting the pioneers.
3. **Geographic level:** about 100 local chapters (= regional groups) have sprung up across the globe, everywhere from Finland to Serbia, from Austria to Chile, and from the UK (with initial activities in Totnes, London, Cambridge, Oxford, Findhorn) to San Francisco, USA. They represent the movement at the grassroots level.

4. **Legal level:** the sixteen associations are in the process of founding an international association which will fulfil coordination and supportive functions.

The associations are predominantly member societies but there is also one research association. Four years after it came into existence, the original Austrian founding association now has about 500 members. Half of these are private individuals, while the other half is made up of organizations. The association's homepage also lists four categories of non-material supporters. By late 2014 these included 1,750 businesses, 6,000 private persons, 60 politicians (from various parties) and 7 municipalities/regions.

I. PIONEER GROUPS

Economic pioneers

A core process of the Economy for the Common Good involves pioneer businesses and organizations which:

- draw up the Common Good Balance Sheet voluntarily;
- help to develop the Common Good Balance Sheet with their experience and expertise;
- cooperate with and learn from one another;
- disseminate the idea in various regions and the corporate landscape.

During the first year some fifty enterprises compiled the Economy for the Common Good Balance Sheet as part of a "test run" and were then audited. Valuable experience in regard to the content of the balance sheet as well as the process was gathered in this way. On 5 October 2011, one year after the movement was launched, regional groups of pioneer enterprises addressed the public in seven cities in Italy, Germany and Austria, introducing the movement and announcing the initial results of their Common Good Balance Sheets at decentralized Common Good Balance Sheet press conferences. The media response was overwhelming. The German television broadcaster ZDF, newspapers and magazines such as the German *Spiegel* and the *Süddeutsche Zeitung*, Italy's prominent newspaper *Repubblica* and many more media reported on the event. As was expected, this set off the next wave of development.

By the end of 2014 the number of Common Good enterprises had grown to over 200. In addition to three joint press conferences and the participation of up to 13 cities and regions, local public relations work had been stepped up. In Frankfurt, the first press conference featuring medium-sized companies committed to the Economy for the Common Good project took place, with participants from three countries.

Enterprises may choose between three levels of membership:

- The Common Good Balance Sheet is drawn up on a trial basis, without any external pressure (Level 1).
- The Common Good Balance Sheet is drawn up together with other enterprises in the same peer group. The enterprises evaluate each other (perform "peer evaluation") and are "cursorily" reviewed by auditors. This form of membership is possible for enterprises with a maximum of 50 employees (Level 2).
- The Common Good Balance Sheet is drawn up individually or in a group with or without consultancy and is then audited externally (Level 3).

Pioneer companies that draw up the Common Good Balance Sheet are simultaneously called upon to demand a new democratic process that will lead to a more equitable economic order. Thus their political contribution is very different from the support given by voluntary corporate social responsibility initiatives. Enterprises which, for various reasons, have not yet opted to draw up the Common Good Balance Sheet (for example, because they are waiting for it to become legally binding or wish to meet the new challenge by taking smaller steps) can set a valuable example by supporting and implementing Level 1.

Political pioneers

Now that a first wave of pioneer enterprises has embraced the idea, the body politic has started to take a growing interest in the movement too. Municipalities and cities are suffering from the effects of globalization, competition in attracting businesses, tax competition and the power of financial markets, to ever-increasing degrees. Thus they identify strongly with the notion of the Common Good. Municipalities can become Common Good municipalities through a city council resolution, which enables them to implement a series of projects. For example:

- They can draw up the Common Good Balance Sheet in city-run businesses. The cities of Weiz, Graz, Mannheim and Zaragoza have taken this path. In Weiz this was done in the department of culture, and in Zaragoza the city's company for house building.
- They can invite local private enterprises to draw up the Common Good Balance Sheet and make the results transparent through public files while rewarding participating businesses with public contracts. The Common Good enterprises could be honoured by the municipality once a year, and exemplary services to the common good could be awarded.
- Common Good municipalities could introduce elements of an alternative financial system, for example establish a branch of the Bank for the Common Good, participate in a "Regional Common Good stock market" or introduce a regional complementary currency.

- The first citizen participation process to take place is the development of the Municipal Common Good Index. This is conceived of as an index for quality of life which can be used by municipalities as a basis for later calculating the Common Good Product at the national level. The fifteen to twenty-five quality-of-life indicators to be included in the Common Good Index could be compiled via democratic citizen participation processes, ideally with scientific support.

- The second citizen participation process would be the Municipal Economic Convention. The task of this body would be to formulate the ten to twenty key ground rules for conducting business. Procedural guidelines for holding such a convention have been developed by the Association for the Promotion of the Common Good Economy with widespread participation of its members. Furthermore, guidelines for "municipal monetary conventions" exist: democratic assemblies at the local level which pursue the goal of creating the foundation for a democratic monetary constitution.[2]

- Last but not least, the first established Common Good municipalities could pursue the foundation of Common Good Regions – political districts or quarters (such as, possibly, Mühlviertel, The Black Forest, Grisons, Vinschgau, Apulia, Extremadura, Wales) – which would ideally incorporate all of the respective region's municipalities. With the support of the individual Common Good municipalities, such Common Good regions could induce the province/county/state to become a "Common Good Province/County/State".

The first Common Good municipalities were established in the Vinschgau region of South Tyrol, Italy, under the coordination of the Terra Institute of Brixen; Latsch, Schlanders, Mals and Laas have all drawn up their own

Common Good municipal report. This example has inspired emulation and attracted visitors – among them a delegation from Salzburg's state government, which has adopted promotion of the Economy for the Common Good as a part of its government programme. In Spain, representatives of ten municipalities and cities met in Madrid in autumn 2013, among them representatives from the first two official Common Good municipalities, Miranda de Azán near Salamanca, and Orendain in the Basque Country, Spain. The second, nationwide meeting took place in Seville in late 2014. In Venezuela, a district of the capital city – Chacao – was the first municipality to draw up a Common Good Balance Sheet. A group of Economy for the Common Good experts/ consultants and activists is supporting the municipality, facilitating the establishment of the necessary infrastructures. Now that Local Agenda 21, Climate Alliance and Fair Trade municipalities exist, Common Good municipalities could constitute the next integrative step.

Cultural pioneers

Teachers and professors have introduced the Common Good Economy to educational institutions all by themselves. At an estimated 100 universities, activities of this kind are being carried out in teaching and research as well as in the application and public propagation of the Economy for the Common Good principle. In 2014, the German Ministry of Education approved two research projects on the Economy for the Common Good. Three colleges and universities are already considering setting up an MBA programme focused on the Economy for the Common Good, and a proposal for such a programme will be submitted to the University of Salzburg in 2015. The University of Barcelona has submitted a Chair for the Economy for the Common Good at UNESCO in Paris. I have received awards from two Latin American universities, and the lecture course I gave at the University of Graz received the teaching award for the year 2013. Countless

Bachelor's, Master's and diploma theses as well as dissertations devote themselves to this topic. The same goes for term papers written at schools. The most wonderful news so far is that the business school of the 22nd district of Vienna will establish a school branch devoted to the Economy for the Common Good called the "HAK experience" in the school year 2015/16. This has all evolved through the initiative of countless educators and researchers.

2. SUBSTANTIVE LEVEL: EXPERT TEAMS

Editors

The Common Good Balance Sheet is the core of the model. For this reason many people want to know who decides on the criteria it is based on and how these criteria are weighted in terms of points.

The Common Good Balance Sheet Editorial Team started out as a group of four who volunteered a lot of time and energy to incorporate the feedback of pioneer enterprises, private individuals and organizations, continually improving the balance sheet.

By July 2011 the Common Good Balance Sheet had already been revised twice on the basis of feedback from pioneers and committed citizens. Version 3.0 became the foundation for the Common Good Balance Sheets drawn up in 2011. It was compiled by almost sixty enterprises.

Version 4.0 followed in 2012, and in 2013, Version 4.1. came along. In our opinion, it will take some years before the Common Good Balance Sheet is "finely tuned", which is to say, precise, representative, comprehensible and user-friendly. Not until then will we call upon legislators to create a law which makes the Common Good Balance Sheet binding.

Until then the editorial team will make ongoing efforts to optimize it. There is currently one editor in charge of each Common Good indicator, which means that a total of seventeen editors share the core task. Each of these is assisted by a small circle of experts and interested private persons, as well as representatives of organizations that participate in the further development of individual indicators. The three tasks of these compact teams are: (a) to process the large amounts of feedback, (b) to actively research sustainability standards and reports and (c) to continue creatively developing the indicators on the basis of the information collected.

In 2014 the editorial team renamed itself; it is now called the Matrix Development Team. This team is coordinated by three individuals devoted to the functional principles, the content and the propagation of the Matrix.

Business consultants

Some of the Attac businesspeople were entrepreneurial consultants in the past. Quite a few of them experienced inner conflicts when helping businesses get the better of other businesses through aggressive or egoistic "counter-petition", and assisting them to maximize their financial profit at the cost of everyone else. The Economy for the Common Good solved this conflict of values. Now the consultants can support businesses in efforts to help other businesses, protect the environment and do good for society. This work is more meaningful and gratifying.

The consultants offer various support services for pioneer enterprises. They can:

- draw up Common Good Reports and Common Good Balance Sheets (attending to everything from initial information to the auditing process);
- shape developmental processes that feed into the creation of Common Good businesses by formulating vision statements, developing strategies, organizational development and empathic leadership;

- give expert advice on special criteria such as sociocracy (Common Good Indicator C5), Cradle to Cradle (Common Good Indicator E3) or changing over to an ethical bank (Common Good indicator B1);
- help shape customary consulting fields such as team development, human resource development and quality management using a Common Good orientation.

In the future, consultants will be coordinated by an economic association whose task will be to incorporate internal networking and advanced training, to develop mutual forms of conduct in keeping with the spirit of cooperation and the values of the Economy for the Common Good, and to establish standards for consultancy services. In addition, they will organize seminars which lead to certification in many countries. A further goal will be to ensure Common Good enterprises have access to trained business consultants.

In principle, the process of compiling Common Good Balance Sheets and reports can be executed without any consultant. After all, the movement does not want to create dependencies. All documents, including the Common Good Balance Sheet, elucidations on the indicators, and the template for the Common Good Report, will be freely available and cost-free for everyone. Efforts are being made to acquire a creative-commons licence. Depending on their needs and preferences, pioneer enterprises will be able to draw up a Common Good Balance Sheet individually, in a group, or with professional assistance.

Auditors
External audits serve to check the Common Good Reports and reveal the degree to which the Economy for the Common Good is put into practice in a company's daily business affairs. Similar to audits of financial balances by chartered accountants, Common Good Balance Sheets will

be evaluated by Common Good auditors. Through a well-meaning and factually well-founded outside perspective, firms' self-assessments that are overly positive or excessively critical can be adjusted.

In 2011, 35 businesses that received more than 600 points were audited externally on the basis of the reports and the Common Good Balance Sheets. (Twenty enterprises with fewer than 600 Common Good points were audited by another pioneer enterprise, following the principle of "peer audit"). This procedure entailed comparing the data provided for the reports with the specifications made for elucidating the criteria on the Matrix, with the results being critically but benevolently scrutinized. Via several rounds of feedback it was possible for firms to submit missing data and complete their Common Good Report in this way. The first auditor (each audit process was performed by at least two auditors) awarded a certain number of points for each criterion and issued an audit opinion in the form of the Matrix. This Matrix was easily comprehensible and designed to serve as a learning tool.

Since then, the audit process has been fine-tuned. In the meantime, audits can be conducted at any time. Audit opinions are valid for two years. Small enterprises with 50 employees or fewer can opt for peer evaluation. Depending on the size of the business, auditors make visits at longer or shorter intervals in order to get as comprehensive a picture as possible by talking to the entrepreneurs on site and perusing documents.

Auditing services will also be coordinated by the economic association. The auditors organize certification processes, advanced trainings and quality assurance measures. The audit fees are scaled according to the size of the enterprise. Each auditor receives the same hourly fee and provides some services on an unpaid basis as well.

To keep the costs for consultancy and audits down, we are making efforts to receive funding from the various federal states and other agencies. Fortunately, some pledges to provide funds have already been made in Austria and Germany (Hamburg, Berlin and Brandenburg).

In the long term, it would be desirable if the public sector were to cover the costs of auditing Common Good Balance Sheets, with the proportion of assistance increasing progressively in relation to the result of the balance sheet in question – as quid pro quo for services provided by the enterprise for the benefit of the common good, so to speak.

Later, quality standards and accreditation for auditors could be placed on a legal foundation. It is conceivable that there could be a special chamber of Common Good auditors.

Public speakers

The public's interest in the Economy for the Common Good is enormous. Every day a number of enquiries concerning lectures are made in an increasing number of countries all over the world, including the UK and USA. All segments of society are taking an interest, including businesses, municipalities, universities, schools, trade unions, farmers' associations, environmental organizations, cultural associations, public institutions and ministries and governments. The demand for lectures can only be met with the assistance of a large pool of speakers. Twice a year, training for speakers takes place in Germany, for the moment. The public speakers spread the idea of the Economy for the Common Good in keeping with the principle of "sowing the seed".

Ambassadors

The speakers are supported by prominent ambassadors who promote the idea in the public eye, in associations, at institutions and in political parties. The first ambassadors are Helmut Lind, CEO of the Sparda Bank Munich; Lisa Muhr, co-founder of the eco-fair fashion label Göttin des Glücks, Hilde Weckmann of Märkisches Landbrot in Berlin, and Francisco Álvarez, a journalist and ethical investor from Spain. Noah Schöppel from Augsburg is the first youth ambassador. After the launch of the book in the UK, USA, Canada and Australia, we will be looking forward to finding ambassadors from these countries as well.

Scientists

Across the world, academics in various disciplines have formed networks with an aim of researching the Economy for the Common Good as well as teaching students about it. The first two network nodes were Germany-Austria-Switzerland and Spain-Latin America. The UNESCO Chair project in Spain evolved from the latter. At the University of Santiago de Chile, the "Common Good Accounting" project is being launched. In Vienna, an International Summer University called "Alternative Economic and Monetary Systems" took place, with participation by four universities. It was awarded the Sustainability Award of the City of Vienna in 2014.

A major source of resistance against the Economy for the Common Good is the population's deep-seated belief in the capitalist image of humankind. Many people desire solidarity-based, cooperative behaviour but believe that the majority would not be willing or able to embrace this principle. This belief manifests itself in public discussions time and time again. And yet the assumptions that lie behind the capitalistic view of humankind have, to a great extent, been scientifically disproved. In fact, it would seem that human beings:

- by nature have an inclination to help and cooperate if they are not raised to be competitive;
- have a capacity for empathy, are interested in the welfare of others and take pleasure in it;
- feel the need to be part of a community and wish to make a contribution to its success.

Moreover it appears that:

- groups in which everyone has a say are more productive than hierarchically organized teams;
- groups whose members make mutual decisions on how to distribute profits are more productive than teams in which the bosses or owners make such decisions alone.

These empirically researched sociological and scientific studies are not, however, as well-known as competing social Darwinist myths. Although the latter lack any empirical foundation, they are deeply rooted in our minds. The Economy for the Common Good expert team called Science and Research will compile the socio-psychological, game theory, evolutionary and neurobiological research results, systematize them and then serve up the essence of them in appetizing titbits in order to spread the word. If dogmas are replaced by scientific insight, the seeds of the Economy for the Common Good planted in this way may one day bear fruit. This is a task which can be executed by many people without too much individual effort.

Another way in which the circle of scientists could take action would be to help develop a Common Good Product as an alternative to Gross Domestic Product. So far this only exists as an idea.

Consumers

A very simple contribution which people could make immediately consists of asking businesses they frequent whether or not they have already drawn up a Common Good Balance Sheet, which would provide an important foundation for deciding which businesses to support. Some activists have already done this, and their efforts have borne fruit. Granted, not all businesses follow the motto "The customer is always right" – which is one reason why the Common Good Balance Sheet is so important – but many businesses take the feedback given by their customers very seriously. The goal is to ensure an increasing number of enterprises engage in the process so that eventually it will be in the best interest of all enterprises to draw up a Common Good Balance Sheet. Ideally, enquiries about the Common Good Balance Sheet would come not only from customers but also from banks, investors, public authorities and co-enterprises who select their business-to-business partners in accordance with their Common Good Balance Sheet results.

3. GEOGRAPHIC LEVEL: LOCAL CHAPTERS

All pioneers and experts can work together in regional "local chapters" synergistically to achieve concrete implementation. Local chapters are local or regional groups which implement the Economy for the Common Good in municipalities, cities, districts, counties and large regions. By late 2014 the number of local chapters in the UK, the USA, Austria, Italy, Germany, Switzerland, the Netherlands, Poland, Mexico and Colombia has risen to 100. Committed people can contribute to change anywhere by taking the initiative to build up a local chapter themselves. Comprehensive guidelines are available which provide assistance in doing this.[3] The activities of local chapters comprise:

- contacting, accompanying, supporting and motivating pioneers in business, politics and culture and providing them with expert knowledge and "transformational energy";
- carrying out awareness-raising and educational campaigns by staging public events and offering seminars or coaching sessions;
- conveying "methods of co-action" such as sociocracy, systemic consensus, nonviolent communication, dialogue, dynamic facilitation and the Art of Hosting;
- preparing and co-initiating local democratic economic conventions;

- developing individual projects such as the Individual Balance Sheet or a game based on the Common Good Economy;
- contributing new facets to the overall model and process, such as an individual balance sheet, a prototype for democratic conventions or a common good management tool.

4. LEGAL LEVEL: INTERNATIONAL ASSOCIATIONS

Any group of citizens can become active in support of the Economy for the Common Good, but once the group reaches a certain size it earns the right to send delegates to the international parliament of the movement, the delegates' assembly. The first international delegates' assemblies took place in Innsbruck and Munich in 2013 and 2014. They were attended by some 50 to 60 participants from five core states, along with the Netherlands, the USA, Brazil, Bolivia, Peru and other countries.

POSITIVE FEEDBACK (REINFORCEMENT MECHANISMS)

The overall model of the Economy for the Common Good would unfold in a system dynamic similar to that of capitalism. In capitalism, all the professional energy, creativity and motivation is focused on maximizing financial results, and these efforts sustain a particular economic order through countless forms of positive feedback. The Economy for the Common Good would develop a similar dynamic but with the decisive difference that return on investment would no longer be the guiding light; the new guiding light would be the Common Good. Here are some examples of predictable "positive feedback":

- The better the Common Good Balance Sheet of an enterprise, the less this enterprise would have to pay for a loan from the bank.

- Banks would draw up a Common Good Balance Sheet themselves, and enterprises that chose these banks as business partners would improve their own Common Good Balance Sheet by doing so.
- If an enterprise selected its suppliers according to the result of their Common Good Balance Sheets, their own Common Good Balance Sheet would thereby improve.
- If enterprises made sure that their products were only sold by enterprises that had a good Common Good Balance Sheet, their own Common Good Balance Sheet would improve as well.
- If enterprises cooperated with one another, the Common Good Balance Sheets of all participants would improve.
- Municipalities and all other public agencies would give preference to enterprises with good Common Good Balance Sheet results when it came to awarding public contracts.
- Consumers would ask the businesses they frequented whether they had a Common Good Balance Sheet.
- Trade journals would write features on benchmark enterprises with the best Common Good Balance Sheets.
- Consumer magazines would highlight ethical enterprises.
- Job supplements would highlight ethical performers.
- Quality associations of all kinds would place greater store by Common Good Balance Sheets and make membership conditional upon a positive Common Good Balance Sheet.
- Complementary currency initiatives would make the Common Good Balance Sheet a prerequisite for membership.

A plethora of synergy and bullwhip effects would be generated. In market economies there would be a tendency for pools of participants – the Common Good Zone – to grow, whereas those who resisted would come under increasing pressure and find it hard to explain themselves. They would ultimately become so isolated that they would resort to incentive mechanisms and run the risk of insolvency – unless they decided to change.

STRATEGIC NETWORKING

The Economy for the Common Good views itself as one facet in the future mosaic of a sustainable, democratic and humane society. Hence it seeks cooperation with supporters of similar alternative approaches in order to shared learning, as well as to draw attention to and strengthen one another. If people approaching approaches such as solidarity-based economy, creative commons, economic democracy, post-growth economy, shared value, B Corps, fair trade, social business seek each other out and strengthen their mutual efforts, there is a chance that the prevailing paradigm can be toppled. What is important for the increasing number of people turning away from mainstream politics in profound disillusionment is not to have only one alternative, but rather a plenitude of alternatives. Then everyone could participate in those facets of change that suit his or her interests, talents, education and inclinations.

Change takes place on all levels and in all areas of societal and cultural life. Below, a "mosaic of the future" (work in progress), which one might also call the Second Great Transformation,[4] is shown. The Economy for the Common Good is merely one facet of this.

Most of the initiatives are still only seedlings; as yet, none of them are "system-relevant". But if they continue to grow consistently and to generate positive feedback, they can form the sustainable cultural ecosystem of the future. It is, we hope, only a question of time before these alternatives develop the appropriate infrastructures for communication, coordination, cooperation and perhaps also decision-making processes – that foundations for the enhancement of the civil society tackle this task. It will not be easy, but if more and more people concentrate on this task, solutions will present themselves. This is all a

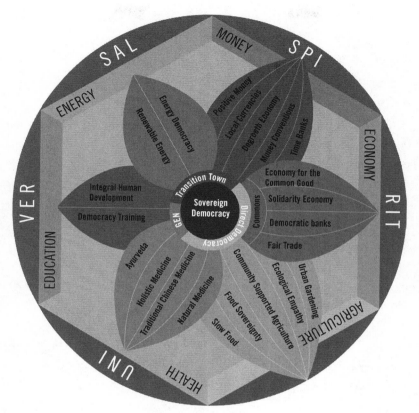

Mosaic of the Future

part of an evolution. And if the new alternatives can learn something from the powerful it is this: cooperation is what counts.

PAVING THE WAY TO THE CONVENTIONS

On the first birthday of the Economy for the Common Good, those involved with shaping its overall process agreed on a five-year strategy. One central long-term goal is to hold economic conventions in several countries. At these conventions the ten to twenty most important ground rules for guiding the economy should be discussed and negotia-

ted democratically and then presented to the sovereign people to be
acted upon. Possible issues are:

- goals and values of the economy
- Common Good Product
- Common Good Balance Sheet
- a Common Good-oriented financial system
- allowed uses of financial profits
- limitations on income inequality
- limitations on inequality of wealth
- distribution of power in corporations
- secure pensions and "democratic dowry"
- reduction of working hours
- leaves of absence
- a categorical ecological imperative.

These are only proposals. The issues for which rules are needed
should be determined democratically as well; in a genuine democracy,
"jurisdiction over jurisdiction" lies with the sovereign people. The
path to a national convention would begin at the bottom: in the
municipalities. This principle has already been described. A "process
design" for how to hold municipal economic conventions is available.[5]
Hopefully, valuable experiences can be gathered from the trailblazers at
the municipal level which can be applied to the large-scale event at the
national level. At the municipal level the citizens could meet once every
two months, for example, in order to:

- get to know each other and familiarize themselves with the
  parameters of the Economy for the Common Good;
- define the ten to twenty questions;
- conduct research and agree on basic issues;
- discuss matters in detail after conducting in-depth research;

- take votes (systemic consensus);
- reflect on results, celebrate and consult on the next steps to take (for example, helping other municipalities).

We expect this process to have several effects:

- Many people would realize that the economy does not follow any laws of nature but rather it follows political rules which can be freely formulated.
- Many people would realize that the rules that currently guide the economy do not conform to their basic values and goals but instead contradict them.
- Many people would develop a longing to have a convention held again at the national level, where the constitution could be reformed – or rewritten.
- Many people would express an emphatic demand for nationwide economic conventions.
- Democracy would experience a welcome surge of vitality. The more widespread the idea of an economic convention became, and the more municipal conventions were held, the more pressure would consequently be put on politicians and parliaments to hold such conventions. A federal convention could be constituted by way of direct elections or delegations from municipal and regional conventions. One pragmatic approach might be to establish a federal convention after at least 100 municipalities had held local conventions and nominated delegates for the federal body.

HOW CAN I PARTICIPATE?

Over the past years I have met a multitude of people who perceive iniquity in the world but have no idea how they could contribute to doing something about it. The Economy for the Common Good offers a plenitude of possibilities for participation. Individuals can:

- found a regional local chapter or support one which already exists;
- adopt one of the fifteen roles which each local chapter consists of (consultant, auditor, editor, speaker, ambassador ...) or invent a new role;
- ask businesses they frequent whether they draw up a Common Good Balance Sheet;
- encourage the enterprise they work for itself to draw up a Common Good Balance Sheet;
- invite the enterprise to learn together with ten to twenty other enterprises in a local pioneer group;
- propose to their residential community that it becomes a Common Good community, and suggest to the region they live in that it become a Common Good region;
- organize a "municipal economic convent" in their residential community, together with other activists;
- integrate the Economy for the Common Good into their own school, adult education centre, college or university;
- network their "favourite alternative" – one they have already committed themselves to – with the Economy for the Common Good, seeking out synergies and building cooperation.

IN CONCLUSION

The Economy for the Common Good constitutes a participatory and open process, seeks out synergies and cooperates with similar approaches such as the solidarity-based economy, the post-growth economy, the global commons, B Corporations, unconditional basic income, the transition town movement, the Blue Economy and others.

The cornerstones of the model as summed up in Appendix 2 do not constitute the demands of the movement but rather food for thought for a democratic process. The only political demand made by the Economy for the Common Good movement is that democratic discussions take place and decisions regarding key elements of the economic order be made in keeping with the needs, values and priorities of the sovereign people. A convention process moving from the municipal and regional to the national and then to the international levels could be a decisive step towards putting the economy and the ground rules which govern it on a democratic foundation.

All human beings who desire such a democratic process are very welcome to participate!

APPENDIX I
Frequently
Asked Questions

Who would monitor the conduct of businesses in terms of their contribution to the Common Good?

Government monitoring would not be stricter than it is today. Minimum standards already exist in many areas. Public health officers, work inspectors, auditors, revenue officers and environmental agencies already check to see if businesses are in compliance with the laws. In essence, nothing would change except that such inspections would cease to be so onerous, since rather than conflicting with the primary goal of the business – the pursuit of profit – monitoring would instead promote it: that is, serving the Common Good.

The Common Good Balance Sheet is a political incentive tool. It would not be monitored by the government. Enterprises would strive to exceed legal standards of their own volition because this would bestow on them advantages and thus help them survive. If they got their above-standard performance documented, they could (a) earn Common Good points and entitlement to government support; (b) win the trust of consumers; and (c) encourage other enterprises to cooperate with them and buy their goods or services because it would be advantageous to do so. The system would finally have the right mechanisms in place!

Maybe it is helpful to compare the Common Good Balance Sheet with financial balance sheets. Corporations have to draw these up in accordance with certain legal requirements (commercial codes, International Financial Reporting Standards) and have them checked externally – by an auditor. Before this happens, certain internal control mechanisms come into play: controlling, revision and compliance. All in all, financial bureaucracy is extremely complicated and much less useful than Common Good Balance Sheets. It involves labelling, billing, accounting, making financial statements, filing taxes, having audits done. Day in, day out, countless people are concerned with monetary bureaucracy, calculating columns of numbers without there being any guarantee that this makes any sense. The aim of the Common Good Balance Sheet is to improve relationships, and for this reason it serves a fundamental purpose. Like a financial balance sheet it would be drawn up in the company – ideally by all employees – and checked ("audited") externally. That's it. The government would have to do nothing besides make it as legally binding as financial balance sheets are today. And later the government would regulate Common Good auditing practices in the way the auditing profession is regulated today.

What incentives for drawing up a Common Good Balance Sheet do enterprises already have?

The more than 200 pioneer enterprises that drew up a Common Good Balance Sheet by late 2014 named the following motivations for engaging in this process: (1) it gave them a sense of social purpose; (2) they utilized the Matrix as a fully fledged organizational tool, allowing for a 360-degree view of all entrepreneurial activities, namely one that is not selectively ethical but, rather, holistic; (3) the Common Good Balance Sheet gave them an opportunity to form a platform for cooperation, which in turn enabled them to help and learn from each other; (4) doing so attracted ethical employees; at pioneer banks the number of unsolicited applications doubled when it became known that they had drawn up a Common Good Balance Sheet; (5) doing so attracted ethically oriented customers and clients; (6) support is already coming in from public sources, even from state governments, and in the near future federal governments will probably start giving support as well (in Austria, four state governments – Vienna, Styria, Salzburg and Vorarlberg – already promote the Common Good Balance Sheet, and in Chile preparations are being made for promoting this practice at the federal level); (7) when "ethical thrust reversal" occurs on the market as a result of reversing the direction which incentives are to take, the competitive disadvantages which currently result from conducting business ethically will be replaced by advantages, and those who are on board first will have the "first mover advantage".

What added value does the Common Good Balance Sheet create which other corporate social responsibility standards do not?

As described in this book, the Common Good Balance Sheet sees itself as the first corporate social responsibility instrument of the second generation, which differs from the first generation in terms of its effectiveness. Why? Because the Common Good Balance Sheet (1) is legally binding, (2) is measurable, (3) is comparable, (4) entails legal benefits or disadvantages (even the best sustainability reports and ethical performances are of little use if those who conduct themselves unethically, and are consequently able to sell their goods and services at lower prices, remain at an advantage). The Common Good Balance Sheet would be embedded in an alternative economic model and constitute a holistic-systemic approach; (5) has a manageable scope and is easy to grasp; (6) is wholly transparent and must be made available to the public; and (7) is audited by an externally assigned professional (first by the movement, later by a Chamber of Common Good Auditors). A second audit would place the results on a more solid foundation.

Wouldn't the obligation to draw up a Common Good Balance Sheet make for overregulation and coercion?

Every law and every form of economy is a form of regulation and coercion. The laws of the Common Good Economy would not be more regulatory or coercive than those of other types of economies, in particular the currently prevailing laws of capitalism. The point is that the current system with all its compulsions has become second nature to us – in fact so much so that we are not even aware of it any more. We will not notice how freeing the change can be until these structural fetters are loosened. Today, we are coerced into presenting a socially prescribed self-image, compelled to be better than others, and encouraged to outsmart them if we can. Whoever lacks sufficient qualifications or has failed to embellish their curriculum vitae with half-truths has little chance of making it on the job market. Whoever fails to make more profit than his competitors must fear for the survival of his enterprise. Whoever has nothing to offer on global markets is already at a fundamental disadvantage. The constraints of the current system are inhuman and ruinous for many. In the Economy for the Common Good the system would generate certain gentle constraints, but if we were motivated by human sympathy and solidarity rather than by egoism and competition, it would not be presumptuous to assume that the majority of human beings would feel more comfortable under this new "guiding light" than in the current regime of imposed egoism.

What would happen to enterprises that did not participate?

They would go bankrupt. Companies that insisted on tolerating child labour in their supply chain, polluting the environment, transferring profits to tax havens, creating miserable working conditions and generating extreme wage differentials would have very poor scores on their Common Good Balance Sheet. As a result, they would end up in the highest tax bracket, have the worst customs classification and the highest interest rates. In turn, their products and services would no longer be competitive. Seen from this perspective, the Economy for the Common Good would be a genuine market economy.

Is there such a thing as one (global) morality?

In essence, this is not even relevant, as the Economy for the Common Good would either grow democratically from below or not evolve at all. Yet the relational values advocated here are globally convergent because they constitute an expression of basic human needs. There is such a thing as an (unwritten) "global ethos".[1] All major spiritual schools and religions advise people to help each other, cooperate, be generous and share! Do not unto others what you would not have them do unto you! This "golden rule" of ethics is universal. I know of no spiritual school or world religion which would teach us to be competitive or egoistic. This makes it all the more amazing that the Western economic system is founded on values that are not supported by any major religion or philosophical school. Rather, social Darwinism, with its scientifically unsound tenets, is the secret religion of the world economy!

Don't we all have our own values?

Regarding some issues, yes, but this does not contradict the collective values that are laid down in legal norms. Every law constitutes a collective decision about values because the ultimate reason for permitting or prohibiting people, for encouraging or dissuading people from doing a certain thing, is ethical in nature. Speed limits and no-overtaking zones serve to protect human life. Protection of private ownership and the thousands of prohibitions, restrictions and limits that are based on this principle are ultimately justified on the grounds of individual liberty. Rules permeate all areas of human life, and every law constitutes the expression of a collective decision on values which imposes its will on all members of a democratic community. We are familiar with most of these laws and they seem self-evident, which is why we often fail to realize that they constitute collective decisions on values which punish us and deprive us of our freedom if we violate them. The art of democracy consists in achieving the maximum possible overall measure of freedom while constraining each individual's freedom as little as possible. I have argued that if we had an Economy for the Common Good, I would expect there to be more freedom in total because all human beings would (a) enjoy sufficient economic affluence to lead a good life; (b) be more able to contribute their skills and talents; (c) get more pleasure out of working and thus find it meaningful; (d) be more at liberty to cultivate interpersonal relationships in business; and (e) have their self-esteem bolstered because the adversarial nature of the workplace would abate and no one would be able to have too much power over others.

Most human beings have a desire for rules based on values for which a consensus has been found: solidarity, justice, democracy, equal liberty for all. Hence the fact that we have laid down laws and enforced constraints which promote values for which there is no consensus – competition, greed, avarice, egoism – seems all the more absurd. In the "free" market economy we are more or less compelled to act egoistically and work against each other if we want to avoid being condemned to failure and ultimately face poverty and exclusion. The compulsion to live according to values for which there is no consensual basis – which is something feared by some, should the Economy for the Common Good be implemented – enslaves us right now, in the capitalistic market economy.

Isn't every human being unique, and isn't capitalism the fairest form of economy for this reason?

We are dealing with a misunderstanding here. The Economy for the Common Good welcomes private enterprises and individual business initiatives because they are an expression of freedom. Private enterprises would be embedded in a different set of goals, however, so that their endeavours would augment the freedom of all rather than endanger it.

In capitalism the "exceptional" status of human beings is very questionable because it unfolds within the framework of an externally dictated set of values. Whoever wins in the race for money, power and success is "unique", but not particularly happy because these values are prescribed ("extrinsic") and not self-imposed ("intrinsic"). For this reason, not even successful people truly feel free in the current system.[2] The Economy for the Common Good also has a certain set of values, but one which, as evidence shows, allow human beings to feel better than they do in a system based on egoism and competition. By lessening the value assigned to money, power and competition, while increasing that assigned to other ("intrinsic") forms of self-fulfilment, as the Economy for the Common Good advocates, human beings would be able to invest their lives with meaning, live in harmony with their individual values, and follow autonomously developed life plans. Such uniqueness does more justice to the multifaceted potential of humankind than the homogenous "individuality" of those who win out in capitalism.

Isn't competition a part of human nature?

As a possible option for behaviour, yes, but not as a compellingly necessary type of behaviour. Competition is an option which our genes allow us to take, but they do not force us to use this option. Similarly, homicide is a possibility, but not a necessity – there is no genetic compulsion to commit murder. Our genes merely "condemn" us to adopting a goal orientation.[3] What really counts, however, is what we learn. The fact that many people do in fact behave in a greedy, selfish and competition-oriented manner today merely proves that the inhabitants of the West have learned these values from an early age. Cultures have existed (and some still exist today, such as indigenous tribes in Colombia) in which cooperation is the customary approach. This tells us very little about human nature in general, but it does tell us a lot about the differences in values and norms between cultures.

The conclusion to be drawn from all this is: just as we, as a cultural collective, have learned to engage in competition and act self-interestedly for decades, if not centuries, we also have the option of systematically learning how to practise empathy, cooperation, solidarity and generosity in the future. This is possible if (a) the value of such ethical conduct is conveyed to us by parents and educators; and (b) we get rewarded for these forms of behaviour in business. This is what it is all about. If we go to the trouble of regulating our collective conduct using laws, then we should ensure that these laws guide us in the right direction, namely in the direction of human virtues, rather than rewarding us for our weaknesses and vices.

Aren't sports proof that competing is fun?

It looks like that at first sight, but if you look closer a different picture emerges. The more it is organized as a game, the more fun sport becomes; the more it is organized as a competition, the less fun it becomes. Games are all *process*-oriented. Those who engage in them can become completely engrossed and forget themselves. In contrast, competition is marked by *goal* orientation. Hence relaxation gives way to stress and pressure. The more we care about winning rather than playing the game, the more fear we will experience instead of pleasure. This might explain why 80–90 percent of fifteen-year-olds in the USA stop going to sports clubs.[4] No wonder. If the winner "takes all" and the others are taunted as "losers", few will find any pleasure in the game. Most of the players will merely be subjected to stress and disparagement. I myself switched from competitive sports to dancing because the contests were accompanied by too much ambition and negative feelings. There was too much focus on the goal rather than on the game, which I love – as an activity. In dance, competition against your partner, as in tennis, is not feasible. And in love, competition works even less. Would it make sense to sleep "against" your partner rather than with him or her, with the objective that whoever reached orgasm first "wins"?!!

Wouldn't it be better if the Economy for the Common Good were founded on intrinsic motivation rather than on "incentives"?

Without a doubt. But that could only be a long-term goal as there are not enough people today who are predominantly guided by intrinsic motivation. Many have learned to pursue external goals and react to external incentives. And more important, if we were to allow enterprises to decide how they wanted to conduct business today, some would undoubtedly adopt a Common Good orientation but others would not, because too many of us have internalized antisocial values such as egoism and competitive behaviour. And these people would win out because the dynamics of the currently prevailing system gives the "competitive edge" to the enterprises with the largest financial profits. This means that the currently existing legal framework for business would have to be eliminated as well!

Is the time ripe for this? As Aristotle said long ago: "If love would reign over the world, all laws would be dispensable." This vision is still valid today! So long as humankind has not reached this stage, we need binding rules. The Economy for the Common Good takes a three-way approach: awareness raising, market-compliant incentives and binding laws. These three approaches would mutually guide us to our goal.

But employees do not want to bear any responsibility, do they?

Shouldn't the employees decide this for themselves? Maybe it really is true that some would not want to bear responsibility. But perhaps some of them would. It makes a difference whether someone is not *allowed* to bear responsibility or if the decision is left up to them. The circumstance that there are currently some people who do not want to bear any responsibility does not provide any fundamental indication of human nature. Otherwise the 69,000 proprietors of John Lewis Partnership would be an unnatural phenomenon, as would the cooperative that has published this book. We are merely being given a historical snapshot here – some bear responsibility, take risks and create jobs, while others "accept" these jobs, bear no responsibility, and take no risks. And we mustn't forget that there are also top managers who do not work for any one corporation for very long, take hardly any risks and sometimes bear no responsibility at all, while there are employees who help build an enterprise and then bear the risk of losing their sole source of income. This risk potentially has a lot more impact than the risk taken by the manager, which is associated with the loss of capital invested by a shareholder, particularly if the employee in question has spent twenty or thirty years of his or her life working for the company and the decades of employment there have shaped his or her identity. In the Economy for the Common Good the workplace would be set up so as to enable the employees of a given company to (a) share responsibility, (b) make decisions democratically, (c) share risks and (d) divide up the fruits of their mutual labour. Enterprises with fewer than 250 employees, for example, would not be forced to do this but would be rewarded if they did. According to empirical studies, groups that distribute the fruits of success amongst all participants equally are likely to perform the best, because appreciating everyone equally provides people with the strongest motivation.[5] Thus one could expect the economy to be more efficient and productive than it is today! Ultimately, by setting such a course the roles of "employers" and "employees" would become blurred and ultimately disintegrate. Since the opposition of interests inherent to capitalism – capital and labour – would be overcome, the intra-societal gulf between "capital" and "labour" would close.

Don't cooperation and competition already coexist? Isn't it a matter of having a balanced proportion?

As previously discussed, evolution is based on the principle of cooperation and the capitalistic form of the economy relies on cooperative structures as well. Families, parents, friends and women do countless hours of unpaid work globally, without which all the male executives and billionaires of the world would not be raised, loved, cared for, encouraged, inspired or appreciated. These are fundamental forms of cooperation which are impeded by economic structures based on competition, structures which are allegedly a part of human nature and hence allegedly cannot be eliminated.

In the market economy itself, cooperation, teamwork and team spirit are actually quite common practices, and yet here cooperation acts as a means to a higher goal – "counter-petition" and contra-operation. Thus, in this framework the relation between competition and cooperation is out of kilter.

Don't legal advantages for those with the highest Common Good orientation and the elimination of competition contradict each other?

At first glance, yes. And yet the Common Good economy would not stoke any customary form of win–lose competition. One key strategy for being successful as an enterprise would be to help other enterprises – by refraining from engaging in aggressive advertising practices, by passing on knowledge and orders, by putting part of one's own workforce at the disposal of others and by providing direct financial support. Besides, a positive Common Good balance would not put a burden on other enterprises; it would benefit them. With structural cooperation of this kind, there would be no "winners" and no "losers". We would have a win–win system. That is the goal. With *no* positive incentives to conduct business in a way that promotes the Common

Good, what is there to prompt businesses to develop in the direction desired by society? The only hope is that they might act on intrinsic motivation, but at present it is simply not sufficient to rely on this alone. At the opposite extreme, minimum legal standards would have to be extremely high and binding for all, but this would entail massive regulatory intervention and ignore the understandable need for a slow and mutual relearning and "transformation". The Economy for the Common Good provides a practical alternative to the pitfalls of these approaches.

If cooperation were rewarded, wouldn't this create monopolies at the cost of the consumers?

This is an understandable apprehension given the logic of our current capitalistic system, which is premised on the assumption that enterprises would ideally like to eradicate all competition in order to milk their customers for all they are worth. In this environment, cartels and secret agreements are a means of increasing profits. But the Economy for the Common Good would not primarily focus on profits. Moreover, uses of profits that proved detrimental to the Common Good would be restricted, as would inequality. For this reason, forming cartels as a strategy for increasing profits would no longer make any sense! Cooperation would exclusively serve to improve an enterprise's Common Good Balance Sheet – and everyone would benefit from this.

What position does the Economy for the Common Good take on the idea of a basic income guarantee (BIC)?

This is one of the most frequently asked questions, and for this reason I will give a very precise answer to it. Let us start with the essentials. The Economy for the Common Good is a developmentally open and democratic process which welcomes all ideas and proposals, incorporating them into the model in an attempt to realize overarching goals such as social protection, human dignity and liberty. Should the elective sovereign deem the BIC to be a suitable measure for achieving the goals of its economic policy, it would be introduced. Inside the movement a series of deliberations have taken place concerning such a proposal:

1. Within the current economic system many people are being marginalized and an unconditional basic income is to be endorsed as a way of preserving their dignity.

2. The system dynamics of the Economy for the Common Good would reverse our priorities, with giving having precedence over taking. Consequently the market would not be dictated by competition and scarcity but marked by cooperation and plenitude instead. There would be enough for everyone.

   a. Everyone who wanted to contribute to reaching this goal through purposeful work would be given the opportunity to do so. Anyone unable to contribute, or at least unable to contribute as much as the others, would receive solidarity income.

   b. Should unemployment arise, it would be minimized by the fact that enterprises would be rewarded for hiring more people and distributing the required workload more equally. All enterprises would participate in solving the economy's problems.

3. In the Economy for the Common Good, core working hours would be reduced to the level desired by the majority of the people, with the average weekly workload somewhere between 20 and 33 hours per week. This way more time would be left for the other key areas of work which round us as human beings, such as cultivating interpersonal relationships and engaging in community work (according to Frigga Haug).[6]

Through the reduction of the average work time alone, unemployment in Austria, for example, could be reduced by two thirds, with the number of job seekers dropping from 300,000 to 100,000.

4. In addition to this, there would be voluntary leaves of absence. Every tenth year of a person's work life could be used for a leave of absence, during which they would receive a temporary BIC, and this would allow that person to focus on other aspects of his or her life. For this type of temporary BIC, two main criticisms of the BIC as a permanent solution would not apply, namely financial infeasibility and resentment from those not receiving a BIC.

    a. If all people took off one year for every ten years of gainful employment, the pressure on the job market would be reduced by 10 percent. This equals the current rate of unemployment in the EU. Unemployment benefits could be channelled into financing for leaves of absence, making the added costs bearable.

    b. When debating the pros and cons of this issue, many people go on the assumption that a large majority of people would pay money into the system and a minority would take it out again. Irrespective of whether this fear is justified, it would become irrelevant if leaves of absence were granted to everyone. Added to which, the experiences we could gather by implementing this measure might allow us to gain new insights into life and work – and create a majority in favour of it.

Would the Economy for the Common Good still be a market economy?

If you try to classify the Economy for the Common Good by assigning it to one of the following economic systems – (1) subsistence economy,

(2) gift economy, (3) market economy, (4) planned economy – it would fit best into the third category. It would constitute a market economy but not of the capitalistic kind we currently have. Rather, it would be a "cooperative market economy". Private enterprises and "free" markets would still exist and generate prices, and money would exist too, as a means of exchange. By their very nature, markets cannot be defined. Markets are places of encounter between people who cultivate economic relations with one another. The ways in which these people treat each other and the ethical and legal rules according to which they shape their relations is just as free as the human spirit, and for this reason such encounters are a matter of democratic creativity and self-determination. The Economy for the Common Good would redefine the foundations on which our prevalent understanding of what a market economy should look like is based. The priority would not be maximization of self-interest but rather maximization of the Common Good. Competition would no longer have precedence over cooperation; it would be the other way around.

Moreover, the Economy for the Common Good would have any number of "commons" such as energy supply companies, schools, railways, postal services and banks. These would not subscribe to the logic of the market but constitute public goods instead. They would not be run by the government, however, but by the population directly. For this reason I have called them "democratic commons".

Third, subsistence would be promoted through a long-term reduction of regular working hours to somewhere between 20 and 33 hours a week. This would result in increased appreciation of other realms of life such as gardening and crafts. The same effect would be achieved by one "year of absence" out of every ten years of gainful employment for each citizen. The Economy for the Common Good would not be a subsistence economy, but elements of subsistence would supplement market activity.

In a similar vein, giving would be promoted in general terms, among other things through accumulation of value. Generosity and sharing would become guiding societal values. If more people engaged in processing goods and manufacturing essential commodities themselves, they could give each other gifts. And there would also be market-compliant incentives for enterprises. If they conducted business in a generous manner and donated resources of all kinds to the community and to other enterprises – from technology and labour to money – they would be rewarded for this.

Even planning elements could be incorporated into the Economy for the Common Good. Enterprises could react to fluctuations in supply and demand in a mutual, solidarity-based manner. The market could be cushioned by a mutually agreed consolidation of supply and demand. This form of market regulation would be decentralized and participative, however, and it would be undertaken by private enterprises themselves rather than by the government. Whoever participated in such measures would be rewarded (there would be no coercion, only incentives). This would reduce the vulnerability to crisis which marks the capitalistic market economy.

A "genuine" type of planned economy which functioned without money and prices because of its strict orientation to needs could be organized in a decentralized, participative and democratic fashion. Internet technology would make this scenario all the more feasible. But such a scenario remains to be implemented. The notion of a "planned economy" continues to be associated with central regulation and dictatorship. And yet any Marxist is aggrieved – and rightly so – when people confuse the reality of the former USSR with the ideals put forth by Karl Marx: democracy, co-determination and human dignity. Whoever is interested in finding out more about sophisticated models of decentralized, democratic planning economies should look at *Parecon* by Michael Albert or the "needs-oriented supply economy" conceived by Albert Fresin.[7]

In short, the Economy for the Common Good draws on various models and all known types of economic system. This is understandable, for none of these is completely bad or entirely good. The trick is to combine the advantages and develop them creatively.

Would an Economy for the Common Good be globally competitive?

Within the current free trade regime, no. Free trade would pose a threat to any "single" Economy for the Common Good. But opening up borders for goods and services – "free trade" – does not serve any purpose per se. On the contrary: free trade (already) poses a threat to our liberal constitutional values and the democratic achievements that are founded on these values: human rights, labour laws, social security, health care, environmental protection and tax equity. If products from countries that fulfil high labour, environmental and tax standards must enter into free competition with products from countries that violate all of these regulations, we undermine our constitutional values and democratic achievements. Free trade constitutes a violation of laws and constitutions if traders do not all adhere to the same preconditions and are unable to agree on a mutual framework for the market. This is exactly what the Economy for the Common Good is proposing: free trade between countries with equal preconditions and standards coupled with protection from countries with lower standards and dumping prices. This would serve to protect democratic achievements and constitutional values.

To put it in concrete terms, enterprises with a good Common Good Balance Sheet would be allowed to trade products customs-free, for example, whereas enterprises with a poor Common Good Balance Sheet would have to pay quite hefty customs duties.

The EU is the largest and most powerful economic zone in the world, and could very effectively press for such alternative global trade regulations if it chose to. Instead, it has joined forces with the USA to push through the current free trade agreement, TTIP[8], an agreement that violates human rights, opposes development and is unsustainable. Even if one could not convince all countries to go along with different regulations, the EU could start with a group of states that was willing to embrace the Common Good principle and create a Common Good zone. This would be a fair-trade zone which could agree upon mutually binding social, ecological and tax regulations, including the two UN Covenants on Human Rights, diverse environmental and climate protection agreements, and measures to promote cultural diversity and avoid tax evasion. This fair-trade zone would also protect itself against countries in which such regulations were not valid. This is a completely legitimate kind of protection.

Would there be growth in the Economy for the Common Good?

As previously discussed, economic growth would not constitute a goal of the Economy for the Common Good per se, and since the success of enterprises would no longer be measured in terms of financial profits, growth of monetary values would no longer be a necessary means of achieving this goal. Money would be reduced to a means of increasing the Common Good, and if less of it were necessary to achieve this, that would hardly constitute a problem. Consequently, one could – it is to be hoped – anticipate permanent growth of the Common Good – health, education, co-determination, quality of the environment and relationships, safety, stability, peace – but not necessarily growth of money, and certainly not growth of natural and material resource consumption, because efficient use of them and their preservation would have become a part of the new goal. The Common Good Balance Sheet of an enterprise would improve to the degree that it:

- manufactured fewer products of no social value;
- required fewer resources along the entire valued-added chain;

- reduced its environmental footprint in terms of waste;
- returned higher proportions of resources to the resource cycle.

This would generate a steering effect in the direction of resource efficiency, recycling, reuse, zero emissions and zero waste. Leverage would be applied – and use of minimum standards, Common Good points and legal incentives would be stepped up – for as long as it took to reduce macroeconomic consumption of resources and emission of hazardous substances to a globally sustainable level.

The Common Good Balance Sheet would not replace all other tools of environmental policy, however, but rather enhance them. In addition it would be necessary to:

- organize a form of global, political resource management which would limit the extraction of natural resources and distribute them on the basis of justice and sustainability criteria;
- instigate a radical ecologization of the tax system;
- mainstream sustainability approaches in all delicate policy fields like agriculture, transport, energy supply, or housing.

Should all measures not suffice, a radical but liberal solution would be the conversion of the use of nature and the consumption of biological resources into a human right, more precisely, into one of the third generation of human rights (after the first generation of political rights and the second generation of economic, social and cultural rights). The idea is as follows. Mother Earth delivers to humanity a certain amount of natural resources and ecosystem services every year. This regular gift could be divided by the total number of human beings and allocated as a global per capita resource budget. In the same way as we successfully coped with the effort to give a financial price to every product and service on the market, we could add an "ecological price" that is paid with the individual's ecological credit card (reloaded yearly). When the year's ecological credit has been "spent", it is no longer possible to buy things on markets with one's ecological credit card. (Of course, mechanisms would have to be implemented to prevent anyone starving or freezing to death.)

Within this equal ecological right for all (liberal approach), everybody is totally free to shape her or his individual lifestyle. Scientists have developed methodologies to measure the ecological impact of every product and service. Of course, this methodology can and should be improved as it is essential for the survival for all human beings on this planet and for a good life for all.[9]

Oxfam expert Kate Raworth has developed the "doughnut model" on this issue.[10] It is a combination of two limitations from the side of the biosphere. The first limitation, the outer circle, is Mother Earth's yearly gift to mankind: the "biological limit". The inner circle marks what all human beings need to consume as a minimum to cover their basic needs: the "social limit". The art of an ecologically efficient economy resides in organizing mankind's consumption of natural resourcs and "ecological footprint" within these two limits: to safeguard simultaneously (social) human rights and the (ecological) rights of Mother Earth. An innovative combination of fundamental rights and market mechanisms could be the following. The per capita comsumption right to the extent of the inner circle becomes an unconditional, non-negotiable and inalienable human right. Whereas the amount between the two circles, the actual doughnut, becomes tradable: thanks to the latter, the poor could sell what they do not need essentially to the rich, and the frugal to the hedonists.

To better understand this idea, it could be helpful to expand the categorical imperative to include the ecological dimension: We should choose a lifestyle that can be chosen by all human beings without the opportunities of other inhabitants of the planet or those of future generations being encroached upon.

The vast majority of scientific research concerning this issue has shown that reducing consumption of resources and material goods need not lead to a diminished quality of life or comfort. On the contrary: if rivers, lakes, forests and fields offered recreational value again; if dwellings required no oil or gas any more because they were well insulated, made of natural materials and intelligently designed (and rich countries stopped warring over resources); if furniture smelled of natural wood and were pleasant to the eye and the touch; if food were healthier and provided us with more energy; if all our essential daily tasks could be performed on foot or using convenient and comfortable public transport; if we all worked in a stress-free environment which allowed for relaxation and enhanced our self-esteem; if poverty and begging on the streets and in public places disappeared because everyone in society and the economic realm had equal opportunities and rights; if everyone could rest assured that their lifestyle did not rob those living in other corners of the globe and future generations of their sustenance, life would simply be better!

APPENDIX 2
Facts, Figures and a Twenty-Point Summary

Initiation of the Economy for the Common Good movement:
6 October 2010

Supporting enterprises: 1,750 (in 35 countries)[1]

Supporting organizations: 220

Supporting persons: approx. 6,000

Pioneer enterprises: 200 (in ten countries)

Local chapters/"energy fields": more than 100 in some 20 countries (including Austria, Germany, Switzerland, Spain, Great Britain and the USA)

Pioneer groups:
- enterprises (business)
- municipalities (politics)
- universities (culture)

Expert teams:
- science and research
- editors

- business consultants
- auditors
- municipal supporters
- public speakers
- ambassadors

Legal entities: Verein zur Förderung der Gemeinwohl-Ökonomie in Austria (founded in July 2011), three additional national associations in Italy, Spain and Switzerland, as well as twelve local associations, for example in Burgenland (Austria), Berlin (Germany), Canary Islands (Spain).

In the process of being founded: an international association

Website: www.ecogood.org/en

TWENTY-POINT SUMMARY

The "model" for the Economy for the Common Good consists of 20 key elements. These do not constitute any definite "positions" or concrete "demands" but rather inspirations for a broad discussion made fruitful by other ideas and alternatives and conducted in a bottom-up democratic process. Economic conventions could take place at the municipal and regional level to start with, then at national levels and perhaps at higher levels after that. The first democratic economic order would evolve as a result of these activities.

1. The Economy for the Common Good would be based on common constitutional values: dignity, solidarity, sustainability, justice, and democracy; as well as values which allow relationships

to succeed: trust, empathy, appreciation, cooperation and sharing. According to current scientific insights, successful relationships are what make human beings most happy and are their greatest source of motivation.

2. The overarching goal of business, i.e., the common good, which is anchored in many constitutions, would be incorporated into the economic order. The legal framework of incentives for business would be reversed, with priority being given to pursuit of the common good and cooperation rather than profit and competition. Enterprises would be rewarded for mutual support and cooperation.

3. Economic success would no longer be measured by (monetary) exchange value indicators in terms of means (profit, return on investment), but rather by (non-monetary) use value indicators in terms of goals (satisfaction of needs, quality of life, the common good). At the macro level (of the national economy) the GDP, as a success index, would be replaced by the Common Good Product. At the meso level (the level of enterprises) the financial balance sheet would give way to the Common Good Balance Sheet. At the micro level, the success of investments would be measured in the ethical instead of financial return on investment, and applications for loans would be subject to a Common Good audit.

4. The Common Good Balance Sheet would be the main balance sheet for all enterprises. The more socially responsible, ecologically friendly, democratic and solidarity-minded an enterprise was, the better its Common Good Balance Sheet results would be. The better the Common Good Balance Sheet results of all enterprises

in a national economy were, the larger its Common Good Product would be.

Enterprises with good Common Good Balance Sheets would have legal advantages such as lower taxes, lower customs rates, less expensive loans, preferential status in regard to public purchasing and research programmes, etc. In this way ethical, environmentally friendly and regional products and services would become less expensive than unethically produced ones, and ethical enterprises would assert themselves on the market.

5. Financial balance sheets would become balance sheets of means. Financial profits would thus become a means rather than a goal and serve to help enterprises reach their new goal, this being to contribute to the common good. As is the case today, it would be permissible to use financial surpluses for real investments (which did not lessen the common good), to pay back loans, to accumulate a limited amount of reserve assets; to pay out a limited amount of profits to employees as well as to grant interest-free loans to other enterprises. It would not be permissible to use surpluses for investments on financial markets (these should cease to exist), for hostile takeovers, for payment of dividends to persons who were not employed in the enterprise (with the exception of the founders), or for donations to political parties.

6. Since profits would merely constitute means but not goals, enterprises could strive to reach an optimal size. They would have no cause to fear being devoured, nor need to keep growing in order to become bigger, stronger and more profitable than their competitors.

7. Since enterprises would be able to adopt an optimal size in a relaxed and anxiety-free manner, there would be many small companies in all sectors. Since they would no longer want to grow, they would find it easier to cooperate with other enterprises and practise solidarity. They would be able to help others out with knowledge, knowhow, orders, employees and interest-free loans, and they would be rewarded for this in the form of good Common Good Balance Sheet results. This would not be at the cost of other enterprises, however, but to their advantage. Counter-petition would be possible but have disadvantages. Enterprises would increasingly form a learning community based on solidarity and the economy would become a win–win system.

8. Income and asset inequality would be limited through democratic discussion and decision-making processes. The maximum income would be limited to ten or twenty times the minimum statutory wage, for example. Private assets could be limited to 10, 20, or 30 million euros and the right to inherit to 500,000 or 1 million euros per person. In cases of family assets the limit could be 10 to 20 million euros per child. Inherited assets exceeding these amounts would be distributed to all descendants of the following generation in the form of a "democratic dowry" via a generations fund. The exact limits would be defined democratically by an economic convention.

9. Corporations exceeding a certain size (for example 250 employees) would distribute rights to vote and partial assets to their employees and the general public step by step. If companies wanted to avoid being progressively democraticized, they could remain smaller. The general public could be represented by directly elected "regional economic parliaments". The

governments at different levels should have no access to or voting rights in public enterprises.

10. The same would hold for the "democratic commons", this being a third category of property alongside a majority of (small) private enterprises and corporations with mixed ownership. "Democratic commons" would be joint operation companies in the education, healthcare, social services, mobility, energy and communications sectors. They would constitute public services.

11. An important "democratic common" would be the Democratic Bank. Like all enterprises, it would serve the common good, and like all "democratic commons", it would be controlled by the democratic sovereign, not by the government. Its core services would be savings, low-cost or cost-free current accounts, inexpensive loans, and participation in regional Common Good stock markets. Nation states would finance their debts primarily via interest-free loans from the Central Bank. The Central Bank would be granted a monopoly on the creation of money, and it would oversee cross-border movement of capital to prevent tax evasion, among other things. Financial markets in the present-day form would no longer exist.

12. In keeping with the proposal made by John Maynard Keynes, global currency cooperation would be established and a global unit of account would be created for international economic exchange. Regional currencies could supplement national ones. To provide protection against unfair trade the EU would establish a Fair Trade Zone (Common Good Zone) in which the same standards would hold for all or customs rates could be oriented towards enterprises' Common Good Balance Sheet results. The

long-term goal would be to establish a global Common Good
Zone on the basis of a UN agreement.

13. Nature would be acknowledged as having an intrinsic value
    and rights of its own, which is why it could not be turned into
    private property. Whoever required a piece of land to live on,
    produce things on or use for agricultural or forestry purposes
    could be provided with a limited amount of it cost-free or for a
    certain usage fee. Provision of such land would be dependent on
    ecological regulations and what exactly it was being used for. This
    would put an end to landgrabbing, large-scale land holding and
    real estate speculation. In return, tax on real estate property would
    be eliminated.

14. Economic growth would no longer be a goal; instead, reducing
    the ecological footprint of individuals, enterprises and nation
    states to a globally sustainable level would be strived for. The
    categorical imperative would be expanded to the use of nature.
    Our freedom to choose the lifestyle we desire would end where it
    started encroaching upon the freedom of other human beings to
    do the same or simply to lead a life in conditions fit for human
    beings. Private persons and enterprises would be encouraged
    to measure their ecological footprint and reduce it to a globally
    equitable and sustainable level.

15. Time spent on gainful employment could be reduced to
    somewhere between 20 to 33 hours weekly on average, as desired
    by the majority. This would free up time for three other central
    areas of work: relationship and care work (care of children,
    ill persons and the elderly), individual work (personality
    development, art, gardening, leisure) as well as political and

community work. As a result of this more balanced use of time, our lifestyles would become less consumption-oriented, more fulfilling and more ecologically sustainable.

16. Every tenth year in a person's working life could be used to take a voluntary leave of absence, which would be financed by an unconditional basic income. During leaves of absence, individuals could do whatever they desired. This measure could reduce the burden on the job market by up to 10 percent. This equals the long-term rate of unemployment in the EU.

17. Representative democracy would be supplemented by direct and participatory democracy. The sovereign people should be able to write the constitution, correct its representation, pass its own laws, vote on international treaties and control areas of basic supply – railways, postal services, banks. In a genuine democracy the interests of the sovereign people and its representatives are identical. The prerequisite for this are comprehensive rights of co-determination and exertion of control by the sovereign people.

18. All substantive cornerstones of the Common Good Economy should be subjected to intensive discussion on a broad basis before being incorporated into a democratic economic convention and compared with alternatives. The sovereign people would have to vote on the final alternatives. All proposals accepted by the sovereign people would be enshrined in the constitution which the sovereign people, and the sovereign people alone, would have the authority to amend at any time.

To enhance democracy, other conventions could be called for issues such as education, media, public services and democracy.

19. For individuals to convey and practise the values of the Common Good from childhood onwards, the educational system would also have to be placed on a Common Good foundation. This would call for different types of schools and different curricula, for example understanding feelings, understanding values, nonviolent communication, understanding democracy, experience of nature, crafts and bodily sensitization.

20. In the Common Good Economy, entrepreneurial success would play a completely different role than it does today and for this reason, different leadership qualities would be asked for. Enterprises would no longer seek out the most ruthless, egoistic, rationalizing and "calculating" managers but rather human beings with a sense of social responsibility, competence and a capacity for empathy, ones who saw co-determination as an opportunity and benefit and thought in terms of long-term sustainability. They would be the new models.[2]

NOTES

Preface

[1] Daly/Cobb (1994), p. 138ff. Dierksmeier/Pirson (2009).

[2] Cf. Sedlaček (2011).

[3] www.ecogood.org/en

One: A Broken System

[1] Bauer (2011), 39.

[2] Smith (1910[1776]), vol. I, 13.

[3] Zamagni / Bruni (2007), 108.

[4] Kant (1998), p. 38.

[5] Cf. Herzog (2013), p. 85.

[6] Hayek (2004), p. 22.

[7] The official name of the economics prize is the "Sveriges Riksbank Prize in Economic Sciences in Memory of Alfred Nobel." It was not one of the original prizes specified in Nobel's will, but rather was added by the Nobel Foundation in 1969.

[8] Kohn (1992), 205.

[9] For instance Chris Barling: "How to Kill the Competition", *Business Matters*, 22 February 2011.

[10] A figure calculated according to the US Department of Labor. The minimum hourly wage was raised to US$7.25 on 24 July 2009 (www.dol.gov/whd/minimumwage.htm). The best-paid hedge fund manager, John Paulson, earned US$ 5 billion in 2010: *Wall Street Journal*, 28 January 2011.

[11] Wilkinson/Pickett (2010), 54.

[12] German Anxiety Index calculated by R+V Insurance.

[13] www.fao.org/news/story/en/item/45210/icode/ and www.fao.org/publications/sofi/2013/en/

14 Jackson (2011), 106.
15 Gallup (2013), 13.
16 Barber (2007), 239.
17 Austrian Chamber of Labour, "Kaufsucht in Osterreich – 2011", study, 24 pp. Available online.
18 Barber (2007), 236.
19 Fromm (1992), 129.
20 Felber (2006), (2008), (2009) and (2012).

Two: Defining the Economy for the Common Good

1 Constitution of Bavaria, Art. 151.
2 German Basic Law, Art. 14 (2).
3 Constitution of Italy, Art. 41.
4 Constitution of Colombia, Art. 333.
5 Constitution of Ireland: Preamble / Art. 6.1 / Art. 43.2.2. / 45.2.ii.
6 Dierksmeier / Pirson (2009).
7 Daly/Cobb, JR. (1994), p. 443 ff.
8 www.happyplanetindex.org/
9 www.oecdbetterlifeindex.org/
10 Enquete Commission "Growth, Prosperity and Quality of Life – Paths to Economic Sustainability and Social Progress in the Social Market Economy" (2013), 28 ff. Available online at http://dip21.bundestag.de/dip21/btd/17/133/1713300.pdf
11 Stiglitz/Sen/Fitoussi (2009).
12 Cf. Felber (2008), 221–38.
13 www.ecogood.org/en/common-good-balance-sheet
14 Thomas Aquinas: "Summa Theologica"
15 Pope Francis, source: www.zenit.org/es/articles/el-santo-padre-un-alcaldedebe-ser-mediador-y-no-intermediario
16 http://ec.europa.eu/internal_market/accounting/non-financial_reporting/
17 Swissinfo, 7 February 2007.
18 Felber (2014a), Chapter 4: "The Foundation: Money as Public Good", pp. 47 ff.
19 Lordon (2010).
20 Redak/Weber (2000), 47.
21 Bakan (2005), 13.

[22] United States, Congress House (1973): *Energy reorganization act of 1973: Hearings*, Ninety-third Congress, first session, on H.R. 11510, p. 248.
[23] *Wiener Zeitung*, 10 June 2008.
[24] Kohr (1995), 43ff.
[25] Nowak/Highfield (2013), 17.
[26] Huckstadt (2012).
[27] Felber (2006), 68–88 and 236–56, cf. also Reimon/Felber (2003), 135–65.
[28] Felber (2014a), pp. 176 ff.

Three: The Democratic Bank

[1] The model for the Democratic Bank was developed by Attac Austria in 2009/10 and launched in June 2010 as an independent project of civil society in Austria: www.mitgruenden.at
[2] Cf. Felber (2012).
[3] Felber (2012), pp. 56 ff. Felber (2014), pp. 87 ff.
[4] See Felber (2012), 73 ff.
[5] Keynes (1980).
[6] Huber/Robertson (2008).
[7] Felber (2014), p. 58 ff.
[8] http://www.positivemoney.org
[9] The author's own calculation following the sovereign-money reform: Thanks to the reform, the Government's debt could be reduced by the size of M1. M1 in UK amounts presently to 87,4% of the public debt.
[10] Date from the Office for Budget Responsibility. Briefing for the House of Commons, 19 December 2014.
[11] Discussed at greater length in Felber (2012), 73 ff.
[12] Keynes (1980).
[13] Stiglitz et al. (2009), 93.
[14] Attac Austria (2010).
[15] For detailed information on the Bank for the Common Good Project go to www.mitgruenden.at

Four: Property

[1] Gurria said: "The gap between rich and poor has widened further since the crisis (...) The issue is not one about inequality, but one about inequalities": www.oecd.org/about/secretary-general/l20-

summitinequality-and-inclusive-growth.htm. Klaus Schwab demanded a reduction of the difference between managers' salaries and the lowest incomes to a ratio of 1:20 or 1:40. Source: *Frankfurter Allgemeine Sonntagszeitung*, 20 January 2013.

2   According to Thomas Piketty, the average real return on investment has been near 8 percent since 1945. Piketty (2014), 202, 435 and 448.

3   Wilkinson/Pickett (2010).

4   John Thornhill: "Income inequality seen as the great divide", *Financial Times*, 19 May 2008.

5   *Stern*, no. 48, 22 November 2007.

6   When the systemic consensus principle is used, several proposals can be voted on, with resistance being measured rather than consent. The proposal which elicits the least resistance is accepted. For more detailed information go to www.sk-prinzip.eu/

7   Wilkinson/Pickett (2010), 268.

8   "Tuition fees: Three quarters of students won't be able to pay off their Debt" , *Independent*, 18 November 2014.

9   Herrmann (2010), 167.

10   Hartmann (2002) "Born to Be a Manager", Interview with Michael Hartmann, *Der Spiegel online*, 26 March 2003.

11   Inspired by Gil Ducommun's "maturity dowry" in Ducommun (2005), 131ff.

12   Philip Faigle, "Rettet die Erbschaftssteuer", *Zeit online*, 4 December 2009.

13   *Results of the financial accounts of the German economy as a whole from 1991 to 2008*, Statistische Sonderveroffentlichung vol. 4, German Federal Office of Statistics and German Central Bank, Frankfurt am Main, June 2009.

14   Pirmin Fessler/Peter Mooslechner/Martin Schurz/Karin Wagner: "Das Immobilienvermogen privater Haushalte in Osterreich", in *Österreichische Nationalbank: Geldpolitik & Wirtschaft*, 2nd quarter, 2009, 113–35; Martin Schurz/Beat Weber: "Die soziale Hangematte der Reichen", MO no. 16/2009. www.sosmitmensch.at/site/momagazin/alleausgaben/37

15   "The case for death duties. How to improve an umpopular tax, *The Economist* 25 October 2007.

16   Piketty (2014), 503.

17   *New York Times*, 14 February 2001.

[18] Mill (1909), II.2.19
[19] Reimon/Felber (2003) and Weizsacker/Young/Finger (2006).
[20] Felber (2006), 257ff. and Felber (2008), 304ff.
[21] Bollier / Helfrich (2013).
[22] Ostrom (2011) and www.onthecommons.org/magazine/elinor-ostroms-8-principles-managing-commmons
[23] According to Austrian law it would be possible to grant nature the status of a legal person. De lege referenda: § 285b ABGB.
[24] Constitution of Ecuador, Art. 71-74 "Derechos de la naturaleza".

Five: Motivation and Meaning

[1] Layard (2009), 46.
[2] Nickerson/Schwarz/Kahnemann (2003), 531–6.
[3] *ORF online*, 4 June 2010.
[4] Bauer (2011), 31.
[5] Bauer (2008), 61.
[6] "Die Mittelklasse irrt", Interview with Richard Wilkinson in *Die Zeit*, No. 13, 26 March 2010. www.zeit.de/2010/13/Wohlstand-Interview-Richard-Wilkinson
[7] Semler (1993).
[8] Joseph Rowntree Foundation/New Policy Institute (2014), 26 and 28.
[9] Eurostat: http://epp.eurostat.ec.europa.eu/statistics_explained/index.php/Unemployment_statistic
[10] Haller (2006); Bakan (2005); Fromm (1992), 146.
[11] *Financial Times Deutschland*, 7 May 2007.
[12] *Der Standard*, 19 September 2009.
[13] "Nonviolent communication" is illuminating in this respect; see Rosenberg (2003).
[14] Roth (1998).

Six: Advancing Democracy

[1] www.einsteinjahr.de/page_2727.html
[2] http://corporateeurope.org/revolvingdoorwatch
[3] http://archive.corporateeurope.org/observer8/brittan.html
[4] http://www.euractiv.com/sections/euro-finance/bowles-blasted-overmove-city-307924

5   http://corporateeurope.org/revolving-doors/2014/10/hill-refuses-givemeps-details-his-past-lobbyist

6   www.businessinsider.com/these-6-corporations-control-90-of-the-mediain-america-2012-6?IR=T#ixzz3QVA5PI4h

7   www.motherjones.com/tom-philp

8   www.globalresearch.ca/gmo-researchers-attacked-evidence-denied-and-apopulation-at-risk/5305324

9   www.insm.de

10 http://maplight.org/us-congress/bill/111-hr-977/359058/totalcontributions; http://maplight.org/us-congress/bill/111-hr-1207/360297/total-contributions

11 Rousseau (2000[1762]), 93.

12 Rousseau (2000[1762]), 81.

13 www.mehr-demokratie.de, www.ig-eurovision.net, www.volksgesetzgebung-jetzt.at

14 Mehr Demokratie (2006), 16.

15 *ARD Panorama*, 12 May 2005: http://daserste.ndr.de/panorama/media/euverfassung100.html

16 In late 2014, the Californian Senate improved the Ballot System. Amongst other improvements, a higher barrier of admission should be implemented in order to focus on few, but broadly supported propositions.

17 The Field Poll, Release no. 2393, 29 September 2011.

18 Forsa/*Stern*.de, 27 December 2006.

19 Crouch (2008).

20 Felber (2014), 38.

21 Hafner (2009).

22 Attac: "10 Principles for A Democratic Treaty": www.attac.at/euconvention

23 *Der Spiegel*, 25 August 2003.

24 Efler/Hafner/Vogel (2008), 122.

25 Josef Proll: "Projekt Osterreich", Speech by the Finance Minister, 14 October 2009, 27.

26 www.superfund.com/HP07/download/press/BP0209.pdf

27 http://ec.europa.eu/internal_market/finservices-retail/docs/capability/members_en.pdf

Seven: Real World Examples

[1] Bauer (2008) 153.

[2] Jeantet (2010), 49.

[3] www.luc.edu/faculty/dschwei/

[4] Karl Marx: *Zur Kritik der Politischen Ökonomie*, Franz Duncker, Berlin, 1859, preface.

[5] www.sekem.com

[6] www.goettindesgluecks.com

[7] One example of criticism: www.soas.ac.uk/news/newsitem93228.html

[8] Felber (2006), 165–84.

[9] www.semco.com.br/en/

[10] www.good2work.com/article/5487

[11] http://de.wikipedia.org/wiki/Ricardo_Semler

[12] www.newfarm.org/features/0104/csa-history/part1.shtml

[13] Kraiss/Van Elsen (2008).

[14] www.agcensus.usda.gov/Publications/2007/Full_Report/Volume_1,_Chapter_2_US_State_Level/st99_2_044_044.pdf

[15] www.buschberghof.de

[16] www.farming.co.uk/news/article/9320

[17] www.regionalwert-ag.de

[18] www.gls.de

[19] www.gemeinschaftsbank.ch

[20] www.abs.ch

[21] www.sparda-m.de

[22] www.bancaetica.it/

[23] www.febea.org/

[24] www.gabv.org/

[25] www.oikocredit.org/site/at

[26] www.johnlewispartnership.co.uk/; the source text cited here was slightly revised for this publication.

[27] www.gugler.at, www.vonderwiegezurwiege.at

[28] www.sonnentor.com

[29] www.badblumauermanifest.com

[30] www.zotter.at

[31] www.ccss.jhu.edu/pdfs/CNP/CNP_At_a_glance.pdf

[32] www.urban.org/UploadedPDF/413277-Nonprofit-Sector-in-Brief-2014.pdf

33 http://nccs.urban.org/statistics/quickfacts.cfm
34 http://data.ncvo.org.uk/a/almanac14/fast-facts-3/
35 http://nccsdataweb.urban.org/NCCS/extracts/nonprofitalmanacflyerpdf.pdf
36 www.ivr.org.uk/ivr-volunteering-stats/176-how-many-people-regularlyvolunteer-in-the-uk
37 Prognos Ag, *Der Spiegel online*, 19 November 2008.
38 Vaughan (2002).

Eight: Putting it Into Practice

1 The term "autopoietic" designates a system capable of creating, reproducing and maintaining itself.
2 Felber (2014), pp. 257 ff.
3 www.ecogood.org/en/general-information/ecg-movement/local-chapters
4 "Great Transformation I" has been shaped by Karl Polanyi. This formula refers to the disembedding of the globalizing economy from its local contexts and adopting a different – capitalistic – ethos.
5 www.ecogood.org/download/file/fid/178

Appendix I

1 Kung (2010).
2 Kasser/Cohn/Kanner/Ryan (2007), 14.
3 Kohn (1986/1992), 25.
4 Ibid., 92.
5 Ibid., 49.
6 Haugg (2009).
7 Albert (2006), Fresin (2005).
8 Cf. Felber (2014b).
9 Cf. for example Aubauer (2011).
10 www.oxfam.org/en/grow/video/2012/introducing-doughnut-safe-andjust-space-humanity

Appendix 2

1 All figures are correct as of December 2014.
2 https://www.ecogood.org

BIBLIOGRAPHY

Albert, Michael (2006): *Parecon. Leben nach dem Kapitalismus*, Trotzdem Verlag, Frankfurt am Main. First published in 2003 as *Parecon: Life After Capitalism* by Verso, London/New York

Alt, Franz/Spiegel, Peter (2009): *Gute Geschäfte. Humane Marktwirtschaft als Ausweg aus der Krise*, Aufbau-Verlag, Berlin.

Altvater, Elmar (2006): *Das Ende des Kapitalismus, wie wir ihn kennen. Eine radikale Kapitalismuskritik*, Westfälisches Dampfboot, Münster.

Attac Austria (2010): "Die demokratische Bank", Project Paper, 6pp., Vienna, May 2010. Available online at www.attac.at/fileadmin/_migrated/content_uploads/Demokratische_Bank_02.pdf

Aubauer, Hans Peter (2011): "Eine wirtschaftlich und sozial verträgliche Ressourcenwende", in *Zeitschrift für Sozialökonomie*, no. 170/171, October 2011, pp. 31–9.

Bakan, Joel (2005): *The Corporation. The Pathological Pursuit of Profit and Power*, Free Press, New York.

Barber, Benjamin (2007): *Consumed! Wie der Markt Kinder verführt, Erwachsene infantilisiert und die Demokratie untergräbt*, C. H. Beck, Munich. First published as *Consumed! How Markets Corrupt Children, Infantilize Adults and Swallow Citizens Whole*, W. W. Norton, London/New York.

Bauer, Joachim (2006): *Prinzip Menschlichkeit. Warum wir von Natur aus kooperieren*, Hoffmann und Campe, Hamburg.

Bauer, Joachim (2008): *Das kooperative Gen. Abschied vom Darwinismus*, Hoffmann und Campe, Hamburg.

Bauer, Joachim (2011): Schmerzgrenze. Vom Ursprung alltäglicher und globaler Gewalt, Blessing, Munich.

Bollier, David / Helfrich, Silke (2013): The Wealth of the Commmons: A World Beyond Market and State, Levellers Press, Amherst.

Brodbeck, Karl-Heinz (2002): *Buddhistische Wirtschaftsethik. Eine vergleichende Einführung*, Shaker Verlag, Aachen.

Crouch, Colin (2008): *Postdemokratie*, Suhrkamp, Frankfurt am Main. First published in 2004 as *Post–Democracy*, Polity Press, Cambridge.

Daly, Herman E./Cobb Jr., John B. (1994): *For the Common Good. Redirecting the Economy towards Community, the Environment, and a Sustainable Future*, 2nd, expanded edn, Beacon Press, Boston.

Darwin, Charles (1859): *On the Origin of Species by Means of Natural Selection or the Preservation of Favoured Races in the Struggle for Life*, John Murray, London.

Dierksmeier, Claus / Pirson, Michael (2009): "'Oikonomia Versus Chrematistike', Learning from Aristotle About the Future Orientation of Business Management", *Journal of Business Ethics* 88:417–30.

Dittmar, Vivian (2014): Gefühle & Emotionen. Eine Gebrauchsanweisung, Verlag V. C. S. Dittmar, Munich.

Duchrow, Ulrich/Bianchi, Reinhard/Krüger, René/Petracca, Vicenzo (2006): *Solidarisch Mensch werden. Psychische und soziale Destruktion im Neoliberalismus – Wege zu ihrer Überwindung*, VSA, Hamburg.

Ducommun, Gil (2005): *Nach dem Kapitalismus. Wirtschaftsordnung einer integralen Gesellschaft*, Verlag Via Nova, Petersberg, Germany.

Efler, Michael/Häfner, Gerald/Huber, Roman/Vogel, Percy (2008): "Europa: nicht ohne uns! Abwege und Auswege der Demokratie in der Europäischen Union", VSA, Hamburg. English version: www.mehr-demokratie.de/fileadmin/pdf/2012-11-23_Europe_not_without_the_people.pdf

Eisenstein, Charles (2011): *Sacred Economics. Money, Gift, and Society in the Age of Transition*, Evolver Editions, New York.

Felber, Christian (2006): *50 Vorschläge für eine gerechtere Welt. Gegen Konzernmacht und Kapitalismus*, Deuticke, Vienna.

Felber, Christian (2008): *Neue Werte für die Wirtschaft. Eine Alternative zu Kommunismus und Kapitalismus*, Deuticke, Vienna.

Felber, Christian (2009): *Kooperation statt Konkurrenz. 10 Schritte aus der Krise*, Deuticke, Vienna.

Felber, Christian (2012): *Retten wir den Euro!*, Deuticke, Vienna.

Felber, Christian (2014a): *Geld. Die neuen Spielregeln*, Deuticke, Vienna.

Felber, Christian (2014b): TTIP – Alle Macht den Konzernen? Hanser, Munich. An English summary ("Alternatives to TTIP, CETA and Free

Trade") is available online: http://www.christian-felber.at/schaetze/
Alternatives-to-TTIP-Christian-Felber.pdf

Fresin, Albert (2005): *Die bedürfnisorientierte Versorgungswirtschaft. Eine Alternative zur Marktwirtschaft*, Peter Lang, Frankfurt am Main.

Friedman, Milton (2006): *Kapitalismus und Freiheit*, Piper Taschenbuch, 3rd edn, Munich/Zurich. First published in 1962 as *Capitalism and Freedom* by University of Chicago Press.

Fromm, Erich (1992): *Haben oder Sein. Die seelischen Grundlagen einer neuen Gesellschaft*, dtv, Munich. First published in 1976 as *To Have or to Be?* by Harper & Row, New York.

Gallup (2013): *State of the American Workplace 2013*, Washington, DC.

Gehmacher, Ernst/Kroismayr, Sigrid/Neumüller, Josef/Schuster, Martina (eds.) (2006): *Sozialkapital. Neue Zugänge zu gesellschaftlichen Kräften*, Mandelbaum, Vienna.

Giegold, Sven/Embshoff, Dagmar (2008): *Solidarische Ökonomie im globalisierten Kapitalismus*, VSA, Hamburg.

Gottwald, Franz-Theo/Klepsch, Andrea (1995): *Tiefenökologie. Wie wir in Zukunft leben wollen*, Diederichs, Munich.

Groll, Franz (2009): *Von der Finanzkrise zur solidarischen Gesellschaft. Visionen für eine zukunftsfähige Wirtschaftsordnung*, VSA, Hamburg.

Gruen, Arno (2005): *Der Verlust des Mitgefühls. Über die Politik der Gleichgültigkeit*, dtv, 6th edn, Munich.

Häfner, Gerald (2009): "Das Potenzial Direkter Demokratie. Durch Beteiligung der BürgerInnen zu besseren politischen Entscheidungen". Lecture given at the Haus der Musik, Vienna, 12 November 2009. Download transcript at: http://vimeo.com/7617007

Haller, Reinhard (2006): Interview in *Der Standard*, 23 December.

Hartmann, Michael (2002): *Der Mythos von den Leistungseliten. Spitzenkarrieren und soziale Herkunft in Wirtschaft, Politik, Justiz und Wissenschaft*, Campus, Frankfurt am Main.

Haugg, Frigga (2009): "Die Vier-in-einem-Perspektive. Eine Utopie von Frauen, die eine Utopie für alle ist", available at www.vier-in-einem.de/

Hayek, Friedrich August (2004): *Der Weg zur Knechtschaft*, Deutsche Reader's-Digest-Ausgabe, Friedrich August von Hayek Institut, Vienna. First published in 1944 as *The Road to Serfdom* by Routledge, London.

Hayek, Friedrich August (2005): *Die Verfassung der Freiheit*, Mohr Siebeck, 4th edn, Tübingen. First published in 1960 as *The Constitution of Liberty* by University of Chicago Press.

Herrmann, Ulrike (2010): *Hurra, wir dürfen zahlen. Der Selbstbetrug der Mittelschicht*, Westend, Frankfurt am Main.

Herzog, Lisa (2013): *Freiheit gehört nicht nur den Reichen. Plädoyer für einen zeitgemäßen Liberalismus*, C. H. Beck, Munich.

Holzinger, Hans/Robert-Jungk-Bibliothek Für Zukunftsfragen (2010): *Wirtschaften jenseits von Wachstum? Befunde und Ausblicke*, Zukunftsdossier No. 1, Lebensministerium, Vienna.

Hopkins, Rob (2013): *The Power of Just Doing Stuff. How Local Action Can Change the World*, UIT Cambridge Ltd., Cambridge.

Huber, Joseph/Robertson, James (2008): *Geldschöpfung in öffentlicher Hand. Wege zu einer gerechteren Geldordnung im Informationszeitalter*, Verlag für Soziale Ökonomie, Kiel. First published in 2000 as *Creating New Money: A monetary reform for the information age* by the New Economics Foundation, London

Hückstädt, Bernd (2012): *Gradido. Natürliche Ökonomie des Lebens. Ein Weg zu weltweitem Wohlstand und Frieden in Harmonie mit der Natur*, Institut für Wirtschafts-Bionik, Künzelsau.

Jackson, Tim (2011): *Wohlstand ohne Wachstum*, oekom Verlag, Munich. Originally published in 2009 as *Prosperity without Growth. Economics for a Finite Planet*. Earthscan/Routledge, London.

Jeantet, Thierry (2010): *Economie sociale. Eine Alternative zum Kapitalismus*, AG SPAK Bücher, Neu-Ulm.

Joseph Rowntree Foundation/New Policy Institute (2014): *Monitoring Poverty and Social Exclusion 2014*, York.

Kant, Immanuel (1998): *Groundwork of the Metaphysics of Morals*, trans. Mary J. Gregor, Cambridge University Press.

Kasser, Tim/Cohn, Steve/Kanner, Allen/Ryan, Richard (2007): "Some costs of American corporate capitalism: A psychological exploration of value and goal conflicts", *Psychological Inquiry* 18, pp. 1–22.

Keynes, John Maynard (1980[1943]): "Proposals for an International Clearing Union", *Collected Writings*, Vol. 25: *Activities 1940–1944*, Cambridge University Press, pp. 168–95.

Klimenta, Harald (2006): *Das Gesellschaftswunder. Wie wir Gewinner des Wandels werden*, Aufbau-Verlag, Berlin.

Knoflacher, Hermann (2006): "Zähmung des Kapitalismus? Warum wir die Religionen brauchen", in Hermann Knoflacher/Klaus Woltron/ Agnieszka Rosik-Kölbl (eds.): *Kapitalismus gezähmt? Weltreligionen und Kapitalismus*, echomedia, Vienna, pp. 40–69.

Knoflacher, Hermann/Woltron, Klaus/Rosik-Kölbl, Agnieszka (eds.) (2006): *Kapitalismus gezähmt? Weltreligionen und Kapitalismus*, echomedia, Vienna.

Kohn, Alfie (1992): *No Contest. The Case against Competition. Why we lose in our race to win*, Houghton Mifflin, Boston/New York.

Kohr, Leopold (1995): *Small Is Beautiful. Ausgewählte Schriften aus dem Gesamtwerk*, Deuticke, Vienna.

Korten, David C. (1995): *When Corporations Rule the World*, Kumarian Press/Berrett-Koehler, West Hartford/San Francisco.

Korten, David C. (2015): *Change the Story, Change the Future. A Living Economy for a Living Earth*, Berrett-Koehler Publishers, Oakland.

Kraiss, Katharina/Van Elsen, Thomas (2008): "Community Supported Agriculture (CSA) in Deutschland", *Lebendige Erden*, 2, 44–8.

Küng, Hans (2010): *Projekt Weltethos*, Piper, Munich.

Kurz, Robert (2000): *Marx lesen. Die wichtigsten Texte von Karl Marx für das 21. Jahrhundert*, Eichborn, Frankfurt am Main.

Kurz, Robert (2005): *Schwarzbuch Kapitalismus. Ein Abgesang auf die Marktwirtschaft*, Ullstein Taschenbuch, 4th edn, Berlin.

Kymlicka, Will (1997): *Politische Philosophie heute. Eine Einführung*, Campus, Students' Edition, Frankfurt/New York. International Student Edition of *Contemporary Political Philosophy* first published in 1994 by Oxford University Press.

Latouche, Serge (2007): *Petit traité de la décroissance sereine*, Mille et une Nuits, Paris.

Layard, Richard (2009): *Die glückliche Gesellschaft. Was wir aus der Glücksforschung lernen können*, Campus, Frankfurt/New York. First published in 2005 as *Happiness: lessons from a new science*, Penguin, London.

Lordon, Frédéric (2010): "Ein Würfelbecher namens Börse. Alle halten Aktienmärkte für nützlich und unentbehrlich, aber das ist ein Mythos", *Le Monde diplomatique*, 16 February 2010.

Marx, Karl (1872): *Das Kapital. Kritik der politischen Ökonomie*, Voltmedia, special edition, Paderborn. First published in English in 1887 as *Capital: critique of political economy*.

Mehr Demokratie (2006): *Praxis, Tipps + Argumente 2006*, pamphlet, 59 pp., 6th edition, Munich.

Mies, Maria/Shiva, Vandana (1995): *Ökofeminismus. Beiträge zur Praxis und Theorie*, Rotpunktverlag, Zurich. First published in 1993 as *Ecofeminism*, Zed Books, London.

Mill, John Stuart (1909): *Principles of Political Economy with Some of Their Applications to Social Philosophy*, 7th edn, Longmans, Green, London.

Nagel, Bernhard (2007): "Wettbewerb und Rechtsordnung", Farewell Lecture at the University of Kassel, 1 February 2007: www.nachdenkseiten.de/?p=2109

Nickerson, Carol/Schwarz, Norbert/Kahnemann, Daniel (2003): "Zeroing in on the Dark Side of the American Dream: A Closer Look at the Negative Consequences of the Goal for Financial Success", *Psychological Science*, Vol. 14, No. 6 (November 2003).

Norberg, Johan (2003): *Das kapitalistische Manifest. Warum allein die globalisierte Marktwirtschaft den Wohlstand der Menschheit sichert*, Eichborn, Frankfurt.

Nowak, Martin A./Highfield, Roger (2013): *Kooperative Intelligenz. Das Erfolgsgeheimnis der Evolution*, C. H. Beck, Munich, First published in 2011 as *Supercooperators* by Canongate, Edingburgh.

Ostrom, Elinor (2011): Was mehr wird, wenn wir teilen: Vom gesellschaftlichen Wert der Gemeingüter, oekom, Munich.

Paech, Niko (2012): *Befreiung vom Überfluss. Auf dem Weg in die Postwachstumsökonomie*, oekom Verlag, Munich.

Piketty, Thomas (2014): *Capital in the Twenty-First Century*, Harvard University Press, Cambridge, MA/London.

Redak, Vanessa/Weber, Beat (2000): *Börse*, Rotbuch Verlag, Hamburg.

Reich, Robert (2008): *Supercapitalism. The Transformation of Business, Democracy, and Everyday Life*, Vintage Books, New York.

Reimon, Michel/Felber, Christian (2003): *Schwarzbuch Privatisierung. Wasser, Schulen, Krankenhäuser – Was opfern wir dem freien Markt?*, Ueberreuter, Vienna.

Rifkin, Jeremy (2006): *Der Europäische Traum. Die Vision einer leisen*

Supermacht, Fischer Taschenbuch, Frankfurt. First published in 2004 as *The European Dream: How Europe's Vision of the Future Is Quietly Eclipsing the American Dream* by Tarcher, New York.

Robertson, James (2012): *Future Money. Breakdown or Breakthrough?*, green books, 2012.

Rosenberg, Marshall (2003): *Nonviolent Communication. A Language of Life*, 2nd edn, Puddledancer Press, Encinitas.

Roth, Gerhard (1998): *Das Gehirn und seine Wirklichkeit. Kognitive Neurobiologie und ihre philosophischen Konsequenzen*, Suhrkamp, Frankfurt am Main.

Rousseau, Jean-Jacques (2000[1762]): *Vom Gesellschaftsvertrag oder Die Grundlagen des politischen Rechts*, Insel Taschenbuch, Frankfurt am Main. First published in English in 1782 as *The Social Contract, Or Principles of Political Right*.

Schönborn, Christoph (2006a): "Referat zu Weltreligionen und Kapitalismus", in Knoflacher/Woltron /Rosik-Kölbl (eds.): *Kapitalismus gezähmt? Weltreligionen und Kapitalismus*, pp. 18–24.

Schönborn, Christoph (2006b): "Gott und der freie Markt", *Viennaer Zeitung*, 22 December 2006.

Sedláček, Thomáš (2011): *Economics of Good and Evil. The Quest for Economic Meaning from Gilgamesh to Wall Street*, Oxford University Press.

Semler, Ricardo (1993): *Das SEMCO-System. Management ohne Manager*, Heyne, Dresden. Published in English in 1995 as *Maverick! The Success Story Behind the World's Most Unusual Work Place*, Grand Central Publishing, New York.

Sikora, Joachim (2001): *Vision einer Gemeinwohl-Ökonomie – auf der Grundlage einer komplementären Zeit-Währung*, Katholisch-Soziales Institut der Erzdiözese Köln, Bad Honnef.

Sliwka, Manfred (2005): *Denkschule Evolution. Führungsintelligenz und Führungsverantwortung in Wirtschaft, Politik und Gesellschaft*, Books on Demand, Norderstedt.

Smith, Adam (1910[1776]): *The Wealth of Nations*, 2 vols., Dent, London.

Steindl-Rast, David (2005): *Die Achtsamkeit des Herzens*, Herder, Freiburg.

Stiglitz, Joseph (2006): *Die Chancen der Globalisierung*, Siedler, Munich. First published in 2006 as *Making Globalization Work* by W. W. Norton, New York.

Stiglitz, Josef et al. (2009): *Report of the Commission of Experts of the President of the United Nations General Assembly on Reforms of the International Monetary and Financial System, Intermediate Report* (early June 2009) for the UN Conference, 24–26 June 2009.

Stiglitz, Joseph/Sen, Amartya/Fitoussi, Jean-Paul (2009): Report by the Commission on the Measurement of Economic Performance and Social Progress, Paris, 14 September 2009.

Tiefenbach, Paul/Nierth, Claudine (2013): *Alle Macht dem Volke? Warum Argumente gegen Volksentscheide meistens falsch sind*, VSA, Hamburg.

Ulrich, Peter (2005): *Zivilisierte Marktwirtschaft. Eine wirtschaftsethische Orientierung*, Herder, Freiburg.

UNDP (1999): *Bericht über die menschliche Entwicklung 1999*, New York.

UNDP (2005): *Human Development Report 2005*, summary, New York: http://hdr.undp.org/reports/global/2005/pdf/hdr05_summary.pdf

Vaughan, Genevieve (2002): *For-Giving. A Feminist Criticism of Exchange*, Plain View Press/Anomaly Press, Austin, TX.

Von Lüpke, Geseko (2003): *Politik des Herzens. Nachhaltige Konzepte für das 21. Jahrhundert. Gespräche mit den Weisen unserer Zeit*, Arun, Engerda.

Weizsäcker, Ernst Ulrich Von/Young, Oran R./Finger, Matthias (eds.) (2006): *Grenzen der Privatisierung. Wann ist des Guten zuviel?* Report to the Club of Rome, Hirzel, Stuttgart.

Wilkinson, Richard/Pickett, Kate (2010): *The Spirit Level. Why More Equal Societies Almost Always Do Better*, 2nd, revised edn, Penguin, London.

Willke, Gerhard (2003): *Neoliberalismus*, Campus, Frankfurt.

Wolf, Winfried (2007): "Treibmittel Öl & Milchmädchen-Logik. Zur Struktur der weltweit größten Konzerne 2005", *Solarzeitalter* 2/2007, pp. 59–66.

WTO (2005): *Understanding the World Trade Organization*, 3rd edn, September 2003, revised in October 2005. Downloadable at www.wto.org/english/thewto_e/whatis_e/whatis_e.htm

Wuppertal-Institut (2005): *Fair Future. Begrenzte Ressourcen und globale Gerechtigkeit*, C. H. Beck, Munich.

Zamagni, Stefano/Bruni, Luigino (2007): *Civil Economy*, Peter Lang, Bern.

INDEX

"democratic commons", 103, 144, 207
"democratic dowry", 91-2, 95, 107, 111, 188; young employees, 46
"democratic supervisory boards", 86
demographic change, 59
dignity, 107, 136
direct democracy, 137-9 dangers of arguments, 134-5; misgivings, 132; SMUD, 101; Swiss, 102
dividends: employee payouts, 39; payouts limits, 43
division of labour, 97; representative democracy, 129
Dornach, 158
"doughnut model", 212
dumping' types of, 11

eco fair trade labels, 152
eco-villages, 145
"ecological price", 211
ecological sustainability, 22
Economy for the Common Good (ECG), 16, 18, 21, 24, 30, 41, 43, 49, 55, 60, 64, 78, 82, 84, 86, 91, 94, 98, 100-1, 103, 106-7, 116, 141, 148, 154, 165, 169, 199, 201, 204, 209; academic networks, 181; consultants, 177-8; "cooperative market economy", 207; dynamics of, 205; financial balance, 36; first birthday of, 187; investment, 44; legal advantages, 33; market form, 50, 206; money role, 46 participation possibilities, 190; planning elements, 208;

political demand, 191;
regional "local chapters", 183;
relationships, 110; Science and Research team, 182; start of, 25; structural unemployment issue, 107; working hours reduction, 205
ecosystems, "performance" of, 13
Ecuador constitution, 104
Ederer, Brigitte, 115
education, 113, 116-21, 142; democratic convention need, 143; external evaluation methods, 143
Einstein, Albert, 122
elites, 133: economic, 125; economic-political merge, 124; representative democracy power, 137; studies on, 90
empathy, 114-15
employee participation, 155
employers, power of, 5; "employer-employee" blurring, 202
Enlightenment, the, 127
Enquete Commission, German Parliament, 19
enterprises, optimal size, 49
environmental policy, tools of, 211; management systems, 28
equality, absolute principle, 105
Erhard, Ludwig, 19
ethical finance, 160
"ethical thrust reversal", 195
European Union, 55-6, 128, 209; Attac proposed constitution, 140; constitutional issue, 139, 141; development of, 138; Financial